1

Vets Helping Vets Anderson:
In Their Own Words
Volume II

Compiled By Angela Mason Lowe

Anderson, South Carolina

2023

VHVA Press

Anderson, SC

ISBN: 9798398745269

Dedication

In memory of my uncles:

Arthur Crocker
(07/16/1934-10/20/1995)
who served in
The United States Marine Corps
and
United States Air Force

Norman Cleveland Mason
(02/27/1937- 10/27/2022)
who served in
The United States Air Force

Both taught me to honor our veterans and love our country.

Foreword

After the VA shut down its Post-Traumatic Stress Disorder (PTSD) sessions, Jesse Taylor stepped up and decided the program was not going to die. He worked with Ellen Russell of the VA who lead the sessions. With her help and guidance Jesse set out and established a group of combat veterans who needed mutual support to fight the PTSD that affected their lives. Fourteen met as a new group on October 14, 2014. Finding a place to meet was a challenge and they eventually ended up in the Elks Lodge on McGee Road in Anderson, South Carolina.

As the group has grown so has the outreach. A few of the members were recruited into the American Legion Honor Guard that is dedicated to performing military honors at a veteran's funeral. The self-help ministry to take care of a few yards of ailing members has grown into a full scale lawn care service for members with health issues and widows of veterans. As a result of increased donations, the organization can provide ramps and medical equipment to veterans in need.

There was a slow but steady growth in meeting attendance and by April 2023, the meetings reached 150 plus attendees. The phenomenal growth requires a new meeting location. Although the organization has strong ties to the Elks Club, a dedicated home with room to grow is needed. Vets Helping Vets Anderson (VHVA) are in the middle of a successful fund raising campaign to finance the new home.

Vets Helping Vets Anderson has another very important function. Every veteran has a story. Every veteran served our great nation in some way and that story needs to be told. VHVA continues to encourage our members to tell their story. Publication of the first volume of *Vets Helping Vets Anderson: In Their Own Words* allowed these stories to be preserved in print. Our history is being lost. Veterans are a small segment of our society. Everyday more and more veterans pass away taking their story with them. As more veterans stepped forward to share their stories, Angela Mason Lowe compiled the second volume of *Vets Helping Vets Anderson: In Their Own Words* and presented it back to us as a labor of love.

Norm Garrett

Acknowledgements

Volume II would not have been possible without the veterans who served, lived these stories, and agreed to be interviewed. We commend the spouses, families and friends whose love and support encouraged them.

A special thanks to Larry and Susan Morelock who proofread the stories with heartfelt admiration. They succeeded in keeping the veterans' voices intact.

The generosity of Joe Walters, Tommy Lowe and Frank and Brenda Sullivan insured every contributor received a copy of *Vets Helping Vets Anderson: In Their Own Words Volume II*.

Table Of Contents

A Man With A Vision

There are three phases that I envisioned for Vets Helping Vets Anderson. The first phase officially started October 14, 2014, when a group of combat veterans and I met regularly at the Anderson, South Carolina Veteran Administration Clinic (VA) for Post-Traumatic Syndrome Disorder (PTSD). We found ourselves back home again and no place to go to receive the support we greatly needed. Ellen Russell, the counselor at the VA informed us that our PTSD group was being discontinued. I went back to talk to her one last time before she retired. Russell encouraged me to continue meeting with the other veterans within the group to offer support to each other.

I weighed the advice she gave very carefully. Several factors were addressed. A place needed to be found where we could meet on a consistent basis if the support group were to be successful. I realized if I started the group, I was confining my personal and family time in retirement to the service of others. The veterans within the VA group needed to be contacted and willing to continue.

After reaching out to twenty-one veterans, fourteen of us shared the same conclusion. Group therapy was working, and we wished to continue together. With a clear objective, we set out to find a consistent place to meet. We tried various veteran organizations to no avail. Either their facilities were used to full compacity, or the liability involved would not allow a group such as ours to hold regular meetings.

Our first meeting ended up being held at the Anderson County Library. Unfortunately, reservations had to be made every sixty days. Reserving the same time and date became impossible. When our group started, none of us knew whether or not it would work out. We did know as veterans that we would definitely give it our best shot. One thing I knew in my heart of hearts: it was something that was needed because I experienced the success of the group at the VA.

Phase Two

Phase two found us searching for a home again. We organized a meeting with the Elks Lodge of Anderson and negotiated. Our Vets Helping Vets Anderson group would meet every Wednesday morning at the Elks Lodge from 10 AM to 11:30 AM and pay a nominal fee that covered the utilities, etc. From that point, we set up our organization with offices such as founder/president, vice-president, treasurer, and secretary. Our mission continued with our original goal: to support each other as combat veterans with PTSD. For the first couple of months, the attendance consisted of fourteen to twenty or so combat veterans.

We all agreed to expand our organization and to include ALL honorable discharged United States of America veterans, regardless of rank, military experience, or branch of service. I had business cards made up with our meeting place address, time and day of meeting and on the back, a place for the member's name and contact number. Cards were to be given out to men and women who served. Many prospective members throughout the community were recognized as veterans from the caps or jackets they proudly wore.

Membership took off. The meetings remained organized yet informal. Veterans passed the mic around the room and were given an opportunity to introduce themselves, tell their branch of service, and say a few words. We averaged around fifty within a couple of years. When COVID struck and all organizations were shut down, we had jumped from seventy or more to around ninety veterans. As restrictions were lifted, around forty-five members returned wearing masks. Gradually with a lot of hard work, the dedicated, like-minded people increased, and we ran a consistent one hundred forty-five for over a year.

Phase Three

One hundred fifty-nine people attended our Wednesday meeting the day I wrote this, May 17, 2023. This brings us to phase three and the vision of having our own place to meet. About five months ago, I had a brainstorm at a meeting with a full house of veterans: I mentioned surely there was someone who would be willing to donate a parcel of land that we could call our own. Land where we would build a large enough facility to house the growing number of vets attending our meetings. Later I received a call from an excited Tharrell Wheeler who told me a veteran by the name of Roy Jeffcoat was donating 3.15 acres in the city of Anderson, South Carolina to our group.

Wheels started turning and again VHVA was met with obstacles. The parcel, located between Bleckley Street and Whitehall Road, required the city council to rezone the single-family residential land to neighborhood commercial. Over half of the VHVA members attended the city council meetings wearing shirts with the Vets Helping Vets' logo. All with a common goal: VHVA, a non-profit organization that seeks to provide support for veterans through meetings and community service was serious about building a home for themselves.

As an Army veteran, I remain steadfast when on a mission and persevere through obstacles to get the job done right. I am joined by a coalition of veterans, community and state leaders who realize that our organizations is becoming the hub among veteran organizations. We work with the others and stay up to date on their services. Organizations throughout the county specialize in different objectives to serve the veteran. They use their unique specialties such as finding a homeless veteran a home, education and/or employment for the veteran, and other needed services.

Our VHVA group is proud to partner with organizations throughout Anderson County to help guide the veteran to what is available for the service they need. Other VHVA members like me continue to use their skills and retirement time serving others in the community. We have a yard assistance team willing to go out to help veterans and their widows physically unable to do it themselves. Some build ramps for wheelchairs and provide transportation if the need arises. We are a diverse group of veterans in age, branch of service, careers, education, and energy level. The common core is the respect and love we hold for our country and each other.

We continue to hold a smaller Monday night support group for combat veterans suffering from life altering PTSD, proving we are consistent with our original goal while expanding our vision. Businesspeople such as contractors, plumbers, big equipment operators volunteer their expertise, many of them veterans, themselves. They believe in our vision for the Anderson community which makes us stand out as leaders throughout the state.

I am seventy-eight years old and like others in the group, have proven I am an asset to my country and the community. As a leader, I understand there will come a day when the torch will be passed to the younger veterans within our group. I am planning for that day, so that the transition will reenforce our group and lessen the chance of losing any of our objectives.

A successful leader must learn to delegate, build trust, and keep a positive attitude. Something VHVA has developed through the years. Veterans walk through our doors and only utter their name and branch of service when the mic is passed. Our camaraderie entices them to attend each Wednesday. Eventually we earn their trust, and they realize they have found a safe place to share their experiences.

The vision for our new home includes a secure and a comfortable place for veterans to meet while continuing with our mission to support each other. A natural walking trail with benches and shaded gazebo where veterans can sit and talk of days gone by while planning for the future. Members feel a kinship with each other and understand what the veterans as a whole have faced.

VHVA is family oriented. Wives have told me how VHVA helped give their husbands a new outlook on life in their retirement. My wife, Sandy Taylor along with Doris

Burdette formed an auxiliary called the Wives of Vets Helping Vets Anderson to support VHVA.

Our top challenges for building our own facility are the passage of the rezoning, ample parking, while leaving the landscape as natural as possible, and fundraising to supplement the funds already dedicated by self-investing veterans throughout the community. I have no doubt that VHVA will obtain their own home and continue to serve the veterans in our community. One day soon this vision will become reality.

Jesse Wade Taylor

A Good Deed Remembered

Every year at this time, the weeks prior to Veteran's day, I read about the political turmoil of the Viet Nam War and the way returning veterans were treated as reported in the media of that day and still repeated over and over to this day. That was not always the case. I tell myself I should write about my experience of being a veteran, returning to the states from Viet Nam. My father, a newspaper writer and city editor, once told me that it is a sad fact the news media is not what they claim to be themselves to be. They are for profit business operations, owned by biased groups. They are out to make money, influence public opinion, and use sensationalism to get our attention.

There has been a lot written about the maltreatment of Viet Nam veterans by protesters upon their return. I do not doubt that some of those reports are true. But not all of us were greeted by signs, disdain and insults. I am a Viet Nam veteran; I spent a year as a helicopter pilot flying missions in what was called the Delta. I left Viet Nam on a flight one day and late at night the next day arrived at McGuire AFB in New Jersey. I cannot describe the feeling we all had when we took off and climbed up to a safe altitude, or upon landing back in the United States. It was an odd feeling. A mixture of happiness and sadness. We were safe but had left friends behind.

Immediately after getting off the plane a group of us got on a shuttle bus to the Philadelphia Airport. Unfortunately, it was too late for me to get on a flight to Detroit, I am from a small town in northwest Ohio. I booked the earliest flight I could and went outside the terminal to see if there were any hotels nearby. In uniform, carrying a duffle bag I walked up to the head of cab line. I asked the driver if there were any hotels close by, that I wanted to take a hot shower for about eight hours and that I had to be back at seven to catch a flight home. He looked at me and asked if I was just back from Viet Nam, I sighed and said yes. He smiled and said, "I know just the place."

I don't remember the place; it was close and looked expensive. When we got there he was out immediately and had my duffle out of the trunk. I asked him how much I owed. He asked to see my ticket, pulled a card out of his pocket and said to call him in the morning, he would meet me out front and make it one trip. He carried my bag inside to the desk, told the clerk I was just back "from the war" and said to give me a room with lots of hot water, and to wake me up at six so I could take another hot shower and be out front at six thirty. The clerk smiled and said he had the perfect room. As soon as I got in the room there was a knock, room service came in and gave me four or five towels. The guy laughed and said, "You boys back from the war all want a shower, don't they have water over there?" As tired as I was I did take a very long hot shower!

The next morning the phone rang at six am, I got up, and yes, had another shower. While I was dressing the phone rang again to tell me the cab driver was in the lobby to take me to the airport. When I went to pay the bill, the clerk looked at the cab driver and told me since I was after midnight checking in I only owed for the bed linen and the towels, five dollars. I gave him the five and twenty for him and room service. Back in the cab quickly to the airport and again the cab driver is out before I can pay. We are standing on the sidewalk as he hands me my bag. How much I ask. "Nothing" he tells me, "nothing." I looked at him and said I had to pay him something he had been a real help to me. The look on his face slowly changed, I will never forget the how he went from friendly happy to utter sadness. Then In a voice so soft I could barely hear he said, "My sisters boy, my nephew, he didn't come back." I looked at him and I couldn't help it, I started to cry and so did he.

We must have been quite the sight. Two men standing on the sidewalk in the predawn light, crying and hugging, an elderly black cab driver in a dark V neck sleeveless sweater over a long sleeved shirt, wearing one of those old time flat golf hats and a skinny young white (but well-tanned!) Warrant officer in very rumpled khakis. He shook my hand and turned me toward the terminal and told me to get going or I would miss my flight. He was in the cab and gone before the thought that I should have given him something for flowers on his nephew's grave. I will always regret not thinking of that quickly enough.

I believe that the overwhelming majority of Americans love their country, respect the flag and each other. They have no political, religious or racial agenda. They want us all to have a job, a safe place to live, and to be able to care for our families. I saw it that cold October morning, I see it every day.
Anonymous as written: Comanche 33 C Troop 7/1 Air Cav

A Soldier's Story

17 November 1965
Ia Drang Valley, Vietnam

The day before, Colonel Hal Moore and the first of the Seventh Air Cavalry Division troops had been in a successful battle with the Viet Cong. The enemy had been routed. On the following day, the Second of the Seventh Air Cavalry Division was sent in to clean up the battle area. Their job was to pick up any equipment, ordinance, and weapons from the battle and to scout the area for the enemy. *Shiny Bayonet* was a search mission trying to locate a large group of enemy in the jungle.

A message had come over the radio that a B27 air strike had been called for the area and would be on them in a few hours. They were told to evacuate the area and that there were no bad guys in the area. They were told to grab their stuff and move out of there. Each soldier followed the one in front. That was as far as each man could see.

Three hundred and twenty men were marching in an 800-yard-long line into the jungle when they came across three teen-aged Vietnamese at the front of the line. The line stopped. These Vietnamese were interrogated for intel purposes. Unbeknownst to the Americans, there were five men, but two of them had gotten away and were able to inform their army that the Americans were vulnerable. The Viet Cong then surrounded the area, hiding in the thick elephant grass and in the branches of the tall canopy of trees. It was dense jungle and slow going.

At approximately 1:30 in the afternoon, all hell broke loose. Bullets were flying everywhere from ahead and behind. The Americans didn't know where the enemy was. The screams of wounded soldiers filled the air adding more terror to the scene. The hot, humid air pressed down on the soldiers like a sodden woolen blanket. There was little or no water left in canteens.

A 23-year-old second lieutenant named Bud Alley crawled among the wounded keeping his head down as much as possible. He came upon a man he knew from his days at Fort Benning. He recognized Garrett F. Lee. They had played bridge together on occasion. Garrett was bleeding profusely from a wound. Bud had no first aid kit. He called out for a medic. There was so much noise and confusion, no medic answered his cry. Bud told Garrett he would try to drag him to safety, but he was a large man, around 6'2. Bud was 5'8. He straddled Garrett's body and tried to move him, but he couldn't lift him or drag him. Bud realized Garrett was mortally wounded so he knelt down beside him as he died. The battle went on for hours. As night descended, Bud came across other wounded soldiers. He was able to drag and half-carry several men into a ditch and proceed back toward the base camp two miles away. As they neared the camp, Bud told the other men to stay down. "I'll stand up and identify myself. You stay down. I hope they will hear me and let us come into the camp," Bud said. He then stood up and waved his arms. The camp recognized him and told him to come in.

It was the bloodiest one-day battle in the entire Vietnam War. 155 were killed, 134 wounded, out of 320 American soldiers of the second of the Seventh Air Cavalry.

Fall 2022

Nick Gayan, a high school computer teacher, sat at his computer as he had done for many years, searching for any mention of a member of his family who had been killed in Viet Nam in 1965. He was hunting for clues as to how his uncle had died. The family had never been able to get closure. The uncle's name was Garrett F. Lee. Suddenly he came upon an interview on YouTube. It was entitled *Return to Vietnam: Back to Ia Drang (1st Cavalry Division).* As Nick watched the interview with four American veterans of the war, he heard one of the men telling the story of how he had been in the middle of a battle and had been with a wounded soldier as he died. He mentioned that he would never forget the experience of being with the soldier who died. He told the story of trying to drag him to safety but being unable to help him. He said he would never forget the moment when Garrett F. Lee died in his arms.

In November 1965, Garrett's family had gotten the dreaded telegram from the Army telling them that he had been killed. Days later, the casket containing his body arrived for burial. The family had never been able to get any details about how he had died. They had wondered and mourned for fifty-seven years.

Nick was shocked but thrilled to hear his uncle's name and to find out the name of someone who knew what had happened to him. He had to get in touch with Bud Alley somehow.

For days, Nick searched for Bud Alley. He reached out until he finally found Bud Alley. They began to communicate. Nick told his family that he had made contact with a soldier who had known his uncle in Vietnam. Over the months, Nick and Bud formulated a plan for Bud to visit Garrett's family who lived in Iron Mountain, Michigan.

27 May 2023
Iron Mountain, Michigan

A sad mystery was about to be solved. Closure was to come to this family at last. Bud and his wife Caroline and their dog Trudy drove to Michigan to offer comfort to the family of a young soldier who had died in the bloodiest one-day battle of the Vietnam War.

As they arrived at the family home, relatives had gathered to meet Bud and hear the story they had long waited to hear. They gathered outdoors. Bud felt nervous as he walked toward this family. He wasn't sure what he would be able to offer them. He needn't have worried. They sat and listened to Bud tell his story. They were spellbound as he talked. He left out the gory details, but he was able to offer them closure and comfort as he talked.

The next day was Sunday and they moved to a lake house for the day. The family brought food for a giant picnic.

They stood around and talked to Bud and he and Caroline met many of the family. They made new friends and as they left, they knew they had done what they had come to do. As they drove away, it felt good to have been able to help.

Fifty-seven years is a long time to wonder about a loved one's death. But an 81-year-old veteran of a faraway war drove a long way to tell them that someone had been with their son. He did not die alone. Bud had been there and had come to tell them about Garrett F. Lee's last hour.

2023

When Veterans meet, they always ask each other, where were you in the war? They proudly wear their baseball caps identifying their units. They wear jackets and shirts that declare their service. They are part of a strong brotherhood. They salute their flag. They sing the National Anthem.

May we never forget to thank them for their service and for the sacrifices they made to preserve the liberty of these United States of America.

An Khe

The Army built a new military base in the jungle called An Khe near the Thailand and Cambodia borders. Soldiers were sent to support Colonel Hal Moore's First of the Seventh Cavalry Division. Colonel Moore's division had been in Nam for three years. The first of the buildup started with President Lyndon Johnson ordering a troop build-up to win the war. Young soldiers, some fresh from an R.O.T.C. college experience, were put into the Air Cavalry which would use helicopters instead of horses to transport men to and from battle. The army picked men randomly to go. The men of the Second of the Seventh had never been in a helicopter. They had never fired their rifles. Yet, they were sent to war, in a foreign country more than 8000 miles from their homeland. They served. They died. They were scarred.

God bless America and our Soldiers who valiantly serve!

Written by Judy Durham, Foothills Writers Guild member, in honor of her brother Bud Alley, US Army Vietnam War Veteran.

Tommy Bradshaw

My name is Marvin Thomas Bradshaw, SSgt USMC retired. My friends call me Tommy. I enlisted in the U.S. Marine Corps in March 71 in the delay program. I reported to boot camp at Parris Island, South Carolina on June 14, 1971.

Living in Pelzer S.C., I attended Woodman High School. I came from a mixed-up family and did not have a good home. Another family took good care of me until I entered the United States Marine Corps. Their names were Willie and Georgi Rose. I have claimed them as my Mom and Dad ever since. They are now in heaven looking down on me.

Due to my raising, I knew that I had no chance of going to college or for a higher education. I spoke with the Marine Sergeant in Greenville, South Carolina. They had a plan for me to earn a higher education and a good life after all. I learned a lot in a short time, and I am now enjoying myself with the USMC's help.

Once a Marine, always a Marine. I chose the U. S. Marine Corps because of the uniforms and the way they trained you: Ready for anything and any place.

The basic training was tough. Rough from day one. They start breaking you down so they can train you the way they want you to be. The best way to get through basic training is simple, do what you are told to do and do not talk back unless you are asked to speak. The first word is "Sir" and last word is "yes Sir, Sergeant." As long as you follow the rules, you will not have any problems. But most of all, keep your faith in God. He will guide you through, for the **Lord** is on your side.

There are so many things that you have to adapt to. You are not at home or back on the farm letting your parents do all the work. You are doing them yourself, such as: making your bed, cleaning and being at the place where you were supposed to be. You are when, and where, why each minute of the day. DO NOT BACK TALK. They are there to train you for combat and other missions that may come up. They want you ready to react when they say so. I am glad that I entered USMC. It has been a good career.

Once we were "trained" in Okinawa, Japan for two months. We embarked on the Navy ship, USS Anchorage LSD-36. In about two weeks, we set sail. Arrived in Vietnam in February 1972, and left there November 1972.

I was assigned to C Company 1st Marine Division 1st Shore Party Battalion and wore red patches. The unit worked and operated out of Da Nang Air Base. Our job was to assign personnel to the unit in support of supplies. We assisted in moving units to different locations in the areas by use of helo.

There were different types of helos. To name a few: CH-53, CH-46, Chinook, Huey, Observation helos and some other Navy helicopters that we worked with. We also cleared LZ landing zones for the helos to land on. At the time we had no LZ, but we did our job anyway.

Shore Party Marines also operated on the beaches to assist the Navy Seabees on a beachhead by controlling traffic on the beach. Our battalion kept it clear for other traffic and use. In order to tell the difference between the troops, we had

17

a one inch by three inches red patch on our cover and a one inch by one inch red patch on each leg at the knee. Shore Party, was later named Landing Support Battalion (LSB), I was proud to be a red patcher and I still am.

We were there for the withdrawal. The unit had several casualties. Some of my best friends were killed in action and some MIA, missing in action. I remember one, SSGT Jack Smith, U.S. Marine Corps, platoon leader. He was a great marine. I would follow him any time and any place. His name is on the Vietnam Memorial Wall in Washington, D.C.

We all are lucky that some came home in one piece because some did not make it home. Some were killed in action, and some were Prisoners of War. The statement "some gave some, but some gave all" reminds me that war is hell. I was fortunate that I came home safe.

During my career I was on several deployments. The only difference, we were in different places with different people. Always doing what we were trained to do which was to protect the United States of America. We did it with honor. I would do it again if called on. I was not injured physically but was injured mentally. I came home with PTSD and mental problems which I still suffer from today. I have good days and bad days.

When we got home from Vietnam, I felt like all Americans had forgotten who we were. We were treated badly at the airport and told not to wear our uniforms off the plane. There were protesters waiting for us as we stepped off to spit on us and call us names such as baby killer. We had to change from our uniform into civilian clothes in the bathrooms to avoid the protesters.

It was a sad day in America when our troops fought for the freedom of America and the American people. We were sent to Vietnam to do a mission, our job. We did the best we could, but no thanks. Overall, we were treated like a piece of trash upon returning. God bless the Vietnam vets. We all come together when it comes to the support of the American soldier.

While we were on deployment, we were all family. That was the only family you had. We would have parties on the ship and drinking parties at the local bars. Our loved ones back home were miles and miles away. We wanted to be with them. Uncle Sam had other plans for us, so we had to adopt another family. It was called U.S. Marines, U.S. Navy, U.S. Army, etc. This was our/ my family while deployed. We were all for one.

We used to play pranks on each other all the time, but they were done for fun. One prank that comes to mind is a tradition that is done when a ship crosses the equator. The tradition is you are a pollywog if you have never crossed the equator. When you cross the equator, you will become a shellback which is a good feeling afterwards. Some of the things that you must do is eat out of a bowl on the floor with your clothes on backwards and inside out. There are several other things they do to pollywogs to make them a shellback, but this is the fun part.

The six years I spent aboard the USS Mobile LKA 115 consisted of liaison between the Navy and the embarked marines. I was in the "X" Division. My title was Combat

Cargo Assistant. We had one Combat Cargo Officer (CCO). We were the ship's company. The ship could carry two-hundred twenty-six embarked marines. Our main job was to assist the marines on load and off load safely when needed.

We were on board as a ready force if needed anywhere in the world. The ship and the embarked marines were deployed for six months at a time every eighteen months. They also had all their equipment, such as vehicles and supplies, to accompany them. We also did helo operations. The marines departed the ship by helo deck and (LCM-8, LCM-6, LCM-4) small boats that the ship carried aboard. The marines got on to the boats by going down beside the ship on cargo nets. The nets were stored on the main deck and lowered when needed.

After Vietnam I was stationed stateside. My tours took me to several stateside duty stations such as Camp Lejeune, North Carolina; Marine barracks in Bermuda; Camp Pendleton, California; Okinawa, Japan, Mount Fuji, Japan; Burma, Korea, England and several more places. I was awarded several medals and awards and they include the National Defense ribbon, four good conduct ribbons, Overseas Service ribbon, Vietnam Service ribbon, Navy Battle Efficiency 'E' ribbon while on board USS Mobile LKA 115, Foreign Service ribbon, and Kuwait Liberation ribbon.

I served twenty years at active duty and ten years fleet roster (March 1971-March 2001) for a total time of thirty years. During my time in, I learned a lot. I enjoyed the new friends I made and the new families. This is what I needed.

The Marine Corps was and still is my life, along with my lovely wife, Kathy. She is a life saver.

It was not easy coming out after my time period. I had to adapt to the civilian world which was way different from the service. It was like I was a free bird. I still miss the service to an extent. I think of the good times and bad times. I am glad that I served, and I would do it again if called on. I love the United States of America and I always will. The Marine Corps is the best branch.

The advice that I would give to anyone going into military service would be to select the service branch you want. All branches are different, and they do different missions. The best thing to remember when you select the military branch you want to serve in, is to go and do your best. Do what you are told to do. It is and was an honor for me to serve this country. Your military service should be an honor for you.

My best advice to ones that are getting out of the service is to make plans and do your homework. The Marine Corps has taught me to respect and honor other people, have patience, and love one another no matter the color of skin.

I learned how to communicate with other people. Without that you are useless. You have to communicate with people to make the world turn. I learned that I did not have that before entering service. I do a better job now since I have experience, the best kind of training and education.

I hope I can teach others to understand the importance of leadership. Helping them to understand others and to let them know that they are not the only people out there in this world.

The word freedom is an important word. Those who served in the U.S. military paid the price for you and me to be able to have freedom in this country today. Without the U.S. military soldier there would be no freedom. There are people in this nation that do not understand that this is America. The nation I fought for. I want it to stay free, but we are losing our freedom a little each day. God bless America.

We may ask to what extent the civilians know about the service. It used to be that family and civilian friends were proud that their sons went off to fight for their country. It was an honor to do that. Now it's like, "Let someone else do it." When you go in the military, you sign on the dotted line that you will do and serve your country in any way they see fit. That includes: in rain, sleet, snow or any conflict/war. You belong to the United States Military.

I had a few bad habits while serving in the military like going out to bars, getting drunk, and trying to get back to the right ship. I left that behind and I have not had a drink in fourteen years. My life is so much better now, and I am happy about that.

There are some things I miss about my years of service. I miss seeing the places that I visited. Seeing and being with the marine soldiers that I knew then. They were like brothers and a family to me. We had a lot in common, like the love for our country and the freedoms we have. Together, we shared the good and bad times but mostly there were good times.

Every soldier has do's and don'ts of how to transition out of the military. When you went to boot camp, their goal was to wash your brain clear of the civilian world and replace it with their training and education. After serving twenty years or any amount of time in service, it is difficult to say one day, "I am a civilian." The soldier has to clear their mind again to become a civilian once they get out. It is an adjustment of body and mind to say the least. Family and friends have to learn you are not the same person you were when you left because of what you went through. Things have changed a lot and it is going to take time to adjust to the civilian world. Through it all, you still love your family.

I want my family and children to know I served in the United States Marine Corps with honor for twenty years. I was proud to do my duties to protect the United States of America; to preserve the freedoms we have today. I would do it again if called upon for I am not ashamed of the United States of America. I am a proud American. May God bless America.

Vets Helping Vets Anderson is the greatest group of veterans in South Carolina. The way it started out is that the VA had a group that met at the Greenville VA clinic. They dealt with veterans that had PTSD and combat problems. One Wednesday at the meeting, they informed the vets that the program was discontinued. Jesse Taylor was one of the vets that was attending the meeting. Some days or weeks later, I got a call from Jesse, along with the rest of the group, to see if we wanted to start a group on our own. We all agreed and started at the Anderson County Library. To make a long story short: When VHVA started at the Elks Lodge on October 14, 2014, we had fourteen members. We are up to over two hundred members now.

The VHVA is a group of veterans from all branches of service with all ranks that meet together every Wednesday. We started out as a PTSD/Combat veteran group. We now allow all veterans as long as they have a DD214 with an honorable discharge. We are leaning toward and encouraging more of the younger veterans of conflicts.

There is a group that meets on Monday that is just for PTSD/Combat vets. I want to thank Jesse Taylor (founder) and his board members that keep us going strong. We have outgrown our building and are now working on a place to call our own. This group is a godsend to Anderson. It has helped all members with problems. God bless Vets Helping Vets Anderson.

My story is dedicated to my lovely wife Kathie Bradshaw. I am thankful to Kathie's faith in me and God who has kept me alive. Without them, I would not be able to write my story.

It is my opinion that the VA is here to help the veterans but doing a poor job at it. My thanks to the VA Anderson and the DAV, American Legion Post 14, but most of all my wife Kathie. They are responsible for getting my 100% disability. It took me five years, but I finally got it. A little word of advice when dealing with the VA, stay on top of them.

Sergeant Marvin T Bradshaw retired. Go USMC!

Jimmy Burdette

My name is Jimmy (Jim) Burdette, Sr. I was raised in the town of Iva. A small town about twenty-five miles South of Anderson, South Carolina. The population was approximately 2500 souls at the time I was being drafted. It seems like every young man of draft age in Iva was called up. This was in 1966.

My grandparents were dirt poor. Neither set ever owned a car or owned a home. I remember the outhouse because there was no indoor plumbing. Slop jars under the bed for nights and stormy days. The white privilege skipped my family.

My father taught me my sister and brother good work habits and honesty. The first job I remember having was around twelve years old shining shoes at a barber shop near Jackson cotton mill. When I got my driver's license, I also stocked shelves at Cal Erwin's grocery store, cut grass, and ran a paper route. While other kids were playing, I was working. In high school I worked at cliffs cafe flipping hamburgers when the football games were over.

After I received my draft notice, I talked with my father who fought in World War II as to what I should do. My father fought with the 179th Infantry 45th Division. He entered service after the 45th Division landed in Anzio, Italy. His unit liberated one of Hitler's death camps. My father was a very proud American Patriot. He was awarded the Croix de Guerre and other medals. His most prized medals were a Combat Infantry Badge (CIB) and a Purple Heart.

My father advised me to "join" the Army to keep from going to Vietnam. I took his advice in 1966 and joined the Army. Why the Army, I do not know. I took my oath of service at Fort Jackson, South Carolina. The next morning buses pulled up to take us to Fort Gordon, Georgia for basic Training. I was assigned to Company B 3rd Battalion 1st Training Brigade.

I took my first airplane ride after basic training from Anderson County Airport on a two-engine prop plane headed to Advanced Individual Training in Fort Sills, Oklahoma for artillery training. This ride was so rough the stewards had to sit down. It hit air pockets and seemed to drop a thousand feet. This scared the crap out of me and was not a good experience for a first airplane ride.

After completion of my training at Fort Sills, I was sent to Giessen, Germany and assigned to C Battery 3rd Missile Battalion 79th Artillery with the Honest John missiles. I had requested the 79th as my duty station when I enlisted because my father and two uncles helped liberate the country from the Nazi's. The Nazi's were one of the most evil governments ever to live on this planet. I served in Germany from 1967-1968.

My government saw fit to pull me out of Germany and send me to Vietnam in 1968. My cousin Ron Burdette and I flew to Vietnam together. We flew from California to Vietnam. The plane was air conditioned. When I arrived in the country, the first thing I can recall as I stepped to the door of the airplane was the stifling heat.

From the replacement center I was assigned to the 1st Infantry Division B Battery 6/15th Artillery. This was in the III Corps area, war zone three. My home base was Lai-Khe. When I arrived at my assigned area in Lai-Khe, the battery was in the field. They told me to find a bunker. The first night I was there, we were mortared. I ran to a bunker, but it was full. I stood outside the bunker until it was over. Then several lizards and I spent the night in the bunker.

Some of the town provinces that were close to the home base were Loc Ninh, Ho Bo Woods, Tan Son Nhut, Tay Ninh, Saigon and Cholon just to name a few that I remember. The worst place I served in was Thien Ngon Special Forces Camp in Tay Ninh Providence. We only had two of our 105's there. The rest were outside of Saigon.

While there, I was injured when something hit me on the back of the head during a mortar attack. I came out of our bunker, which was underground, to assist in returning fire. Why I did not have on my helmet, I do not know. Our medic could not sew me up, so I was sent to the special forces medic who put ten stitches in the back of my head a few days later.

I was in the ammo bunker when the 105 fired over the top of the bunker damaging my ears. The Lieutenant had me and some other wounded flown to Tay Ninh Base Camp to be treated.

I saw Puff the Magic Dragon, a very impressive war machine, in action in the Thien Ngon Special Forces camp. Puff could bring smoke, death, and destruction. I completed my service in Vietnam at the Thien Ngon Special Forces camp. I returned to the "world" in 1969.

I needed a job when I got home. A close friend, Sonny Gray, had just been hired by the Anderson City Police Department. He suggested I apply there also as they were still hiring. It was never my ambition to be a police officer. I just needed a job, and I was hired. I was in the police force for almost 30 years, retiring as a Detective Lieutenant. The last 20 years I spent as a criminal investigator.

It is a privilege to serve as a member of the Campbell Patriots Honor Guard of the American Legion Post 184 in Anderson, South Carolina. We honor our veterans with military funerals. I have been a proud member of Vets Helping Vets Anderson for a long time. Thanks to Jessie Taylor for starting this group.

I have been married to Doris Darby for 54 years. We have three children, five grandchildren, and four great grandchildren. Our son Jimmy, Jr. is a veteran of the U. S. Navy, volunteered for the Anderson County Fire Department, and owner of Burdette Pest Control. Joey is a Captain with the Anderson City Fire Department. Our daughter, Retha is a mother, homemaker, and works for the YMCA in Barnwell. My wife faithfully serves our veterans at our Vets Helping Vets' meetings on Wednesday. I am proud of my family. I have also been a long time Christian, thanks to Jesus Christ.

Bob Collier

My name is Robert Wesley Collier. My friends call me Bob. I was born in Trenton, New Jersey in 1943. Dad had enlisted in the Army Air Corp but was medically discharged with a heart problem. He worked as an auto mechanic. Mom worked for General Motors in New Jersey. I had a sister and brother both younger than me. All have passed away.

Dad moved to Miami when I was twelve to work for Eastern Airlines. Mom did not want to move to Florida. I got a lot of guidance from an ex-cop and school bus driver named Smitty. Good neighborhood families and friends helped to keep me out of trouble.

I did not hang out with kids from school other than some neighborhood friends. I still keep in touch with two of them at Christmas. I attended Trenton, New Jersey area schools up through the eleventh grade and I was an average student. My better classes were auto repair shop and mechanical drawing.

I worked at several weekend jobs during high school, mostly in construction. My best job was working for the owner of a junk yard. He also bought and sold used cars. I would paint the tire sidewalls and floor mats black, test the six and twelve volt car battery cells without a meter. I rotated cars to different car lots in the city and the car auction. Since I lived across town, I was allowed to drive a car home every day.

My mom thought I was too hard to manage so she gave me a choice of staying in school or going into the military. A friend got me involved with Civil Air Patrol in 1960-1961. I became a member of the CAP drill team. The local Air Force Recruiter talked me into finishing school before enlisting in the U.S. Air Force.

In the beginning of my senior year, I went to Florida live with Dad in Miami. Moving there was very good for me. I completed my senior year at the Miami Central High School which At that time was a tech school. Three hours a day, I was in a Refrigeration and Air Conditioning class.

I was not interested in the HVAC business after high school. The school in Miami was much better and friendlier than the schools in New Jersey. I worked part-time in the evenings as a busboy at a popular restaurant in Miami.

While riding with a friend on the back of his motorcycle, we ended up in a wreck. A car turned in front of us at a busy no turn intersection. I went over the trunk of the car, my friend somehow cleared the roof, and we both landed in the middle of the intersection. We were able to go home from the hospital that night. I later bought the bike, a Honda 250cc Hawk, and replaced the damaged fork and shock assembly myself. This became my transportation.

I put off going in the Air Force until October 1962. I was working for Preston Pipelines as a welder's helper. We installed four-inch gas lines along the roadways in and around Miami. I worked there until I went into the military.

I enlisted in the United States Air Force in October 1962. After an easy six weeks of basic training at the Lackland Air Force Base in Texas, I completed my training at the Keesler Air Force Base in Biloxi, Mississippi with the

3409th School Squadron. From November 1962 until November 1963. The Equipment Repairman courses I completed included six months of Light Ground Radio and six months of Heavy Ground Radio. My squadron had a drill team. We had the cleanest WWII barracks and were exempted from KP duty. Our free time was spent on the Biloxi Beach or roller skating at Gulf Port, Mississippi.

After completing training, I was assigned to the 645th Radar Squadron/Air Defense Command at Patrick Air Force Base, Florida. I arrived on base the day President Kennedy was shot in Dallas, Texas on November 22, 1962. The base supported the Cuban Missile Crisis with B-52s, F104s, and U2 jets during that period.

I worked at the 645th Radar Squadron's radio site where I maintained radio and digital equipment for three years. I received my first digital electronic systems training from an RCA Inc. tech-rep. All of this training from vacuum tubes to semiconductors was very helpful for every job I have had after my military service.

I held part-time jobs while at Patrick Air Force Base, Florida. I worked at the base cafeteria, and as a janitor at Cocoa High School, after working my eight hour shift on base. At the Pelican restaurant in Melbourne Beach, Florida, I worked as a busboy washing dishes by hand and as a waiter when the waitresses needed some time off.

While stationed at Patrick AFB, are frequently made trips home to Miami. Wearing my uniform, I hitched a ride, went by Greyhound bus, and later drove my first car. I have flown commercial in uniform to Dallas, Texas; Portland,

Maine; New York City; Philly, Pennsylvania; Orlando, Florida; Miami, Florida; Gulfport, Mississippi; and to New Orleans Louisiana.

I left the military with the rank of E4 and stayed in the Melbourne, Florida area. After my honorable discharge in 1966, I worked at the Radiation Inc., which is now the Harris Corporation in Palm Bay, Florida. I work as a microelectronics tech, and as an assembly line setup tech for assembly of electronic modules used in LEM, Apollo Minuteman, and other spacecraft telemetry systems.

While working at Radiation Inc. from July of 1967 to December 1968, I became a member of Harbor City Volunteer Ambulance Squad. I joined, took the training, and got my ambulance permit from the police department. The members of the squad were great people to work with, and eventually I became a crew chief. Later I was elected the squad treasurer. Our ambulances were 1959 and 1961 converted Cadillac hearses, and a 1968 International van. Being single I would sometimes be on late night duty and go to my job from there in the mornings.

An engineer friend made me aware of an overseas job maintaining electronic equipment installed on Beechcraft QU-22 aircraft being sent to Nakhon Phanom (NKP) Air Force Base, Thailand. Initially I was sent to Elgin Air Force Base in Florida, to get familiar with the equipment on the six aircraft. The planes were shipped out the day before I got there. I went to NKP in December 1968. This was my first time out of the United States. I got there in time for the Bob Hope Christmas Show.

Radiation Inc. employees resided in the town of NKP which was 15 kilometers of dusty unpaved road from the base and next to the Mekong River. We first stayed in a hotel in NKP. Three of us had to temporarily share one room with one bathroom. We all got Bangkok belly at the same time. Not fun!

We had a van and driver that took us to the base and back. We all got our Thai driver's license and some of us even got our own vehicles. I had a four-cylinder Mazda pickup truck. The six aircraft were called Mini-Bats and were assisting other EC aircraft from another Air Force Base. Our project was cancelled in mid-1969.

At the end of the project, I was asked to work at another project at NKP known as Task Force Alpha as a logistics specialist. I also performed maintenance on all the antenna systems and the digital interface equipment as a field engineer until the end of the contract.

In mid1972, Philco-Ford took over the contract with none of us staying due to significant wage reduction for hiring on in country. I had put the system parts inventory on the site IBM 360-65 computer punch cards with the assistance from an United States Air Force computer programmer.

Computer printouts were used to turn over the antenna and digital interface systems to the new contractor. The Government Property Administrator who oversaw the contractor inventories was so impressed and wrote a letter to the Harris Corporation president about my system inventory record keeping and the computer inventory printouts. Remember this is in the early nineteen seventies.

I had a son while in Thailand and later married his mom. When we came back to Melbourne, Florida, she did not adjust well to life there. I filed for divorce and the court awarded custody of my son to her. They went back to Thailand in May of 1973. In June of 1973 I had an offer with the Harris Corporation to go to either South Korea or Viet Nam. I opted for Viet Nam as I knew some of the workers there and was thinking I would be working in Saigon.

When I arrived in Viet Nam, I was sent to Da Nang Air Force Base to work with the crew there. Our overall job was to write maintenance procedures and to train Vietnamese (VN) airmen how to maintain and repair the monitoring equipment installed in EC-47 aircraft. None of the VN airmen or flight crews actually came to our shop at Da Nang. The EC-47 pilots and crew brought the planes up that had defective electronic boards. Our job was to repair and leave the repaired boards on the plane going back. The crew went straight to town after parking the aircraft and came back when it was time to go back to Saigon.

We lived in the city right across the street from the big Catholic Church. We had no trouble from anyone while there. We ate at local restaurants or cooked in our apartment. I bought a 125cc Honda scrambler to get around town and the base.

We were the "only" Americans working on the air base. We had to man the shop twenty-four hours a day for security reasons. We were performing installed equipment pre-flights at night due to the daytime heat. We did not have access to air units to cool the hot aircraft. Our power cart might have been keeping the basic security guards awake during pre-flights. Rockets started hitting outside the base's west perimeter after 2:00 AM each morning. We ended up changing the pre-flights to a daytime period from then on. We only kept one person in the building at night rotating shifts. The base fuel storage area got hit one night. We could see the fire from our roof in town.

One evening at midnight I heard what I thought was rockets and gunfire. I eventually opened the door and looked towards the base perimeter. It turned out to be the lunar new year celebration from off base. Glad I was able to keep my britches clean.

Our building was right across the perimeter road from the bomb dump. It was sabotaged one morning. Explosion #1 rattled our building pretty badly. Light fixtures and ceiling tiles came down on us. We secured the building, and all got our van and pickup and headed down the taxi way to about the middle of the runway when #2 exploded. We were in town when #3 went off. We watched that one from the roof of our apartment building. After things had quieted down, our ex-marine crew member said, "Bob, let's go back to the site and retrieve everyone's personal stuff from the locked file cabinet." We went back and while cleaning out the cabinet, the #4 explosion put us both on the floor again. We got up and finished loading the truck and headed back to town.

Our hanger was severely damaged but the plains in revetments appeared to be OK. We salvaged our contract by moving our shop to an empty hanger down the runway and across from the air terminal. We stripped everything serviceable including wiring, conduit, phone lines, ceiling tiles, and a very heavy fireproof file cabinet to the new building. We were back up and running in about a week. Note: almost every building on base that was not occupied were gutted and items taken were sold on the black market in town. I have told this story to some vets who doubted the bomb dump story saying it only happened in 1968. It did happen. I have pictures and orders for my service at Da Nang.

Anyway, we stuck it out until May 1975. Our manager in Saigon called and told us to destroy documents and evacuate the planes coming up to get us. We drove into town through crowded streets to get personal belongings and got to the already crowded base terminal. The first 727 jet arrived and stopped outside the terminal with the engines still running and the back steps down. Our crew made it onto the plane including U. S. consulate workers. All of us had orphans sitting on our laps. The next flight or flights did not go as well. People had to be pushed off the steps so they could take off.

The plane got off safely. We landed in Saigon after curfew and had police escort into Saigon to a hotel for the night. The next day I caught a commercial flight to Bangkok, Thailand. My ex-wife and son met me in Bangkok at my old hangout, the Sri Guest House, 1 Soi 38 Sukhumvit Road. We got a quick Thai marriage annulment and took care of other documents. Traveling back to the states with a four year old that only knew Thai was a big challenge. He was valedictorian at Walhalla High School, Walhalla, South Carolina and graduated Clemson University with high honors.

Later in Melbourne, Florida, I met up with and married an acquaintance I knew in Da Nang and later adopted her beautiful five year old daughter. As of this week, May 16, 2023, we have been married forty-seven years. Both kids are college graduates and have given us five grandchildren.

I took a job at an appliance repair shop that paid terrible. I quit there and later got hired by Q-Bit Corporation, a broadband RF amplifier manufacturer. There I was an RF technician quality assurance manager and also maintain the parts inventory. It was a small company. A retired Army friend I kept up with in Walhalla, South Carolina thought I might be able to get hired at the Oconee Nuclear Station in Seneca, S.C.

Moved to Walhalla in September 1979. I did not get hired initially, so I worked at a TV Repair Shop in Seneca. I kept the books for the owner, and we split what was left after the bills. I finally got an interview with Duke Energy and was accepted for employment. After six months of training at Charlotte, North Carolina, with young tech school grads, I got to work at the Oconee Nuclear site as an I&E specialist from 1980 to 2000.

I could not get hired initially, so I worked at the Electronic Image TV Repair Shop in Seneca, S.C. I kept the books for the owner, and we split what was left after the bills. I finally got an interview at Duke Energy with the maintenance manager and was accepted for employment. After six months of training at Charlotte, North Carolina, with young tech school grads, I got to work at the Oconee Nuclear site. In 2000, I was asked to work with the reactor and electrical engineering department.

I retired from Duke Energy in early 2003. After my retirement, I volunteered at Oconee Memorial Hospital pushing wheelchairs. I miss being at work. Fortunately, my last Duke Energy supervisor called me and asked me if I wanted to come back to work. I had a contractor friend I met during plant computer upgrades, and he got me on as a contract worker doing my old job with better pay. I went back to my old cube space for ten more years before I retired again in 2013.

From 2005, I have been doing electrical maintenance, weekly mowing, and other work at my church. My Marine grandson finished five years of active duty earlier this year. He got to spend time in Ukraine (pre-war) and later was in Afghanistan during the evacuation. He is currently at the NASCAR Technical Institute in Mooresville, North Carolina. I have attended Vets Helping Vets meetings since April 2022. I have much respect for the vets that have seen combat.

Gary Cooper

My name is Walter Gary Cooper. My mother and sister named me after the actor. I guess that is why my nickname is High Noon. Gary Cooper played as a small-town Marshall in a movie titled High Noon, that was released in 1952. I was born in Seneca, South Carolina, in the Ebenezer community between Seneca and Walhalla. My high school was in the Keowee community and is now used as an elementary school. I graduated in the class of 1965 with twenty-eight other students. I had a baseball scholarship to Georgia Southern. My father and I went down to the draft board and were told that there was no need for me to enroll in college because they were going to draft me because I was single. My father wanted me to go into the Navy because I had two uncles that served in the US Navy during World War II.

We went down to Anderson, South Carolina, to the recruiter station in my father's 1956 Ford Victoria. We normally only went to Anderson to buy clothes from the Sears and Roebuck that was in the corner of Main Street and Greenville Street. The Recruiters' Office was there at the old bus station. A Navy Recruiter said he had no slots available but to talk to his Air Force buddy. The Air Force Recruiter said that he had four slots open on the delayed entry program. If I took four tests and scored an eighty percent, I could go into the United States Air Force. Selective Service drafted me, but I volunteered for the Air Force. My father took me to the car and said that he wanted me to make an eighty percent. I took the tests and made an eighty percent or higher on all four tests and entered the Air Force.

We passed a McDonald's with the golden arches on our way to the recruiter station. The restaurant opened three years earlier in 1962. My father had never bought a hamburger. On our way home, we stopped and ordered a hamburger for fifteen cents, French fries for twenty-two cents, and a milkshake for twenty-six cents. I drove a school bus for two years of high school. The pay was thirty-five dollars a month. I ate hamburgers at Linda's Drive-In of Walhalla, South Carolina, but for my father, the lunch at McDonald's was a treat.

During my senior year of high school, my parents moved to Decatur, Georgia. They let me stay with a cousin, Mike, back in my hometown to finish school. I worked at a gas station, washed cares and anything to pass the time while I waited for my notice to report. I had been fishing the day my dad called me with the news. When I got my notice to report for duty, my father drove up to Walhalla to tell me. I was to report January 1, 1966. My older sister, younger brother and my parents drove me to Atlanta, Georgia, to catch a plane to Lackland Air Force Base in San Antonio, Texas.

We stopped by a country store on the way and got some snacks and things to eat. The hardest moment was when I rode up the escalator in the airport and looked back at my family, who had tried to hold their emotions until I left. I turned around and look back down at them. My younger brother had broken down and was sitting on the floor and my mother was weeping. The 6 o'clock news depressed everyone. No one knew for sure what the next day may bring.

I made a friend in basic from New York named Mike. We were from different parts of the country and different cultures. He was a big city guy, and I was from a small southern town with barely two thousand people. We got along well. He enjoyed listening to my southern drawl. Another friend, who also had a movie star name, Brian Keith, invited me to Mississippi to visit his family. My friend was Black. My dad worked on farms, in the cotton mill, and was a Pentecostal preacher. Although I had never been around many people of color, I remember going to a church where the congregation was Black three or four times when my father preached. This was during the time the news reported racial tensions throughout the south. We did not encounter any problems, and Brian's family treated me as nicely as anyone ever had. Brian, a great guy, died in an auto accident.

During basic, a Drill Sergeant asks me to pick up cigarette butts. I told him I did not smoke. He asked me if I pooped. The rest is history. I became the permanent toilet cleaner. At Lackland AFB basic training, we learned to make beds, learned to march, and learned to zero in our weapons. Because of a spinal meningitis outbreak in 1966 that closed Lackland's base, basic training shortened from six weeks to four weeks. After basic, the Air Force sent me to Chanute Air Force Base in Illinois. I took a course in communication that included Teletype and keypunch entry on now archaic computers. Other places I served were Griffiss Air Force Base in Rome, New York and Minot AFB, in North Dakota. My Temporary Duty Assignment throughout Southeast Asia was communication with covert operatives in Saigon. We were based in Taiwan.

Although I carried a small creek stone and a lucky penny for good luck, while on a mission, I hurt my knee. This caused me problems all my life and eventually led to a total knee replacement and a disability later in life. I completed my four years of service in 1970. I remained on active reserve status for two years, which meant I could have been called back to Nam anytime because of my skill level. When I left the military, I was sad. I had listened to another Air Force guy, and he gave me poor advice. I received the Air Force Commendation Medal and the United States Air Force Zero Defects Citation six times in-person. They pinned all other standard medals on me.

The Air Force made a better person out of me. I realized I was very caring and helpful. I still feel guilty even today knowing what my buddies went through in Vietnam. As part of my mission, I had to tell lies and today I refuse to. I would rather tell the truth and take the consequences. My military training put me on the right path. I could get good jobs without a college education. I went from a poor country boy to a Director of Procurement at Alcoa Fujikura in Duncan, SC, with a 750-million-dollar budget.

I always wanted to live at the beach ever since I was a senior in high school. When our senior trip to Washington D. C. canceled, we went up to the mountains to Lake Becky for our senior trip. My friend Mike's brother carried us down to Myrtle Beach, South Carolina. This was my first time to go to the beach. My mother ironed clothes for folks in the community, saving for my Washington trip that got cancelled. She gave it to me to use on my beach trip. When I saw the beach, I promised myself I would someday live there. When I retired, I moved to Sunset Beach, North Carolina.

It seems the last two or three generations do not realize what the military is or the sacrifices the veterans made so that they can enjoy the freedoms they have. They do not know what it is like to want anything. With how things are going now, unless America gets back down on their knees and prays to God not to destroy us, we are going to be destroyed. This place looks like a picnic compared to what tomorrow in the United States will look like. They need to know what their forefathers did to make our land a great place to live. Know the importance of honesty, integrity, morality, and staying true to their word. The military helped me grow up, gave me a good skill set, and is still a good career today.

No one knows what tomorrow will bring. My son had a great job with Brinks Security and then diagnosed with non-Hodgkin's lymphoma cancer in 2009. He has fought the battle ever since. His son went into the Air Force and became a jet mechanic on a F35 and was number one in his class. He fell and suffered a traumatic brain injury, which led to his medical discharge. My wife, Judy, shares my compassion for our youth and is an adolescent counselor.

I enjoy the comraderies each Wednesday at our Vets Helping Vets Anderson Meeting. Maurice Hastings, a member, invited me about five years ago. I ran into him at the Ingles Grocery Store. He handed me a card. About two years ago, another veteran invited me. He was purchasing materials to build a ramp for a veteran. This was the group I wanted to be involved with. I finally visited and now I am actively involved in trying to help raise money for a new place to meet. I beat the pavement and apply for grants. No other organization even comes close to the volunteer work these veterans do. We help veterans in Anderson, Oconee, Pickens, and Abbeville. A lot of these are young veterans who have served in Afghanistan and more current conflict. They are hurting, need jobs, and would benefit from the fellowship of older veterans who understand what they are going through. VHVA veterans are working together to help make this happen.

Charley Crawford

My name is Charles Eugene Crawford. I have always been called Charley. I was born in Houston, Texas, but I grew up in a small town in southeast Georgia called Jesup. I played ball, worked on my relative's farms around the area, mostly in tobacco and cotton, as well as worked with my Dad in the air conditioning business.

After graduation from high school, I tried the college life, but it did not last long. I dropped out and was drafted almost immediately. I was living at my parent's home when I received my draft notice. I had recently turned nineteen. I reported to the local post office and climbed aboard a bus headed to Jacksonville, Florida to the induction center. After being inducted, we traveled by bus that night to Fort Benning, Georgia and arrived early the next morning. The drill sergeants stepped on board that morning and everyone's life changed.

At the beginning of boot camp, while still in our civilian clothes, I was put on kitchen patrol (KP). I had been in the army for two days and I was involved in a fight in the kitchen while washing dishes. My job was to slide the dish crate into the dishwasher and another soldier raised the dishwasher doors and removed the clean dishes. He thought it would be funny to raise the doors of the dishwasher before it stopped. This blew hot water all over me, so of course I was not amused. We ended up in a fight and other soldiers separated us. The cook assigned the other guy to peel potatoes! I realized then that this was going to be a very different way of life.

I got through basic training after that with little trouble. Another soldier got to that kitchen instigator outside one night while I was on guard duty and gave him a pretty good beating. The next morning the drill sergeant wanted to know what happened, but no one spoke up. We all low-crawled to the mess hall for a week.

I graduated and was sent to Fort Polk, Louisiana for Advanced Individual Training (AIT). I was to be a mortar man. I completed AIT with no problem. I was called aside and asked to volunteer for Officer Candidate School (OCS). That meant extending my time, so I declined. The next step was back to Fort Benning, Georgia. I had orders for Noncommissioned Officer School (NCO). It was a twelve-week course. You could not drop out until after nine weeks. I stayed and became an E5 sergeant.

I was asked to volunteer for Ranger School. That too required an extension and I once again declined. I was still sent along with the ten other guys to a Ranger qualification weekend at Fort Benning, Georgia. We ran obstacle courses, crossed a river on rope, learned about acquiring food when none was available, and went on a night navigation course. Then we sat down and listened to another sales pitch. I declined and wondered if they could order me to go anyway, but they didn't. I got orders to go to Fort Gordon, Georgia for on the job training (OJT).

As I expected, with OJT behind me, my orders to Vietnam were next. I left in March of 1970 to begin my tour. I arrived in Long Binh, processed in and was sent up to I corps to Phu Bai and assigned to E Company, 1/502 Infantry, 101st

Airborne Division. A week-long training was required at Camp Evans, so that was the next stop. With all that completed and my Military Occupational Specialty (MOS) being mortars, I was sent to Firebase Birmingham to be assigned to a mortar platoon. Nothing was available at the time, so I was shuffled between other firebases with the same results. I ended up back at Firebase Birmingham with no job assignment, so I opened ammo canisters and was put in charge of a crew burning the refuge from the outhouse and pulling night guard duty.

One night my platoon sergeant sent for me. I reported to him to find out he wanted me to bring water for him to shower. I was surprised by that request and quickly declined. He informed me of the differences in our rank and told me to get the water. I told him to find a private and it went south from there. The next morning, I was summoned back to the Platoon Sergeant. He told me to get my rucksack, rifle, and go to supply. Pack for five to seven days with food and ammo. I did and went to the Helipad where I was picked up and delivered to a field unit out in the bush.

This was a bit of a surprise. They were not Americans they were ARVNS, Army of the Republic of Vietnam, the South Vietnamese Army. There was an American Advisor and an American Radio Telephone Operator (RTO) on the first mission out which lasted about three days. When we met on the Helipad to return to the field, I was the only American there. The other two had gone.

One more surprise. I spent the next four to five months alone with twelve South Vietnamese soldiers. My job was a

Forward Observer (FO); directing artillery fire, Cobra gunbirds, and whatever else was needed. My life took a drastic change.

I was extremely upset with the job because I did not know these ARVN soldiers. I could only talk to one of them and that was very limited. Not so sure of their loyalty to Americans for they looked like the enemy. I was concerned that we may be mistaken for the North Vietnamese by some other unit and may be fired upon. I was sure I would die with them. I tried multiple times to get transferred to no avail. Then one day, I got a radio call to come back to Phu Bai. I was going to join an American outfit.

After that, my life changed for the better. I went to see the company commander. He said I had enough time with the ARVNS, and they needed an experienced Forward Observer with a small team group. I was fine with that, so I shipped out to join a six-man team. They placed me with the Bravo Company 1/502 Infantry.

We stayed out thirty to forty-five days on each mission, and we traveled deep into the bush. We ran ambushes at night, climbed mountains all day, and set up observation posts; and also weathered the monsoon season. This was a rough life, but I was so grateful to be with Americans again. I found out I was right about the "fight" in an American unit. We walked into an ambush in November up around Firebase Jack. The sniper hit our point man first. He was dispatched in a matter of seconds.

I had eighteen days left in the Army when I was pulled out of my unit. I thought I would go to the rear and wait out my time but that did not happen. I was sent to a group of twelve Americans to act as a FO for the ARVNS again. We would fly out to some hilltop and set up a perimeter. Then the ARVNS would be flown in to receive their artillery pieces and ammo. They provided fire missions for their units in the field all day then break it all down, move it out, and then we were picked up. We did this daily by helicopter. I never knew where we were, just a point on a map, but I believe we may have been out of country. I had been told at the beginning, if needed that were beyond radio contact, so they always kept a bird in the air around us as a relay if needed.

When I had five days left in the army, I was pulled back to Phu Bai to get ready to go home. I had spent a year in training for mortars and I only dropped one mortar down the tube during my entire time in Vietnam. The rest of the time I had been on the other end – amazing how things turn out. I ETS'd, expiration term of service, out of Vietnam and returned to civilian life.

I left Vietnam just after the New Year in 1971 and flew into Washington State. I processed out of the Army with travel money and a few medals: Combat Infantry Badge, Bronze Star, Army Commendation Medal, Air Medal, plus others, also a handful from the South Vietnamese army. I was on my way home with Army duty behind me.

The Army was rough on me, but My training prepared me for what was to come in Vietnam I survived some awful times, but there were still times to laugh and joke around with some good guys. No better man to be with during bad times than an American soldier; especially a 101st Airborne soldier.

You fight for the man beside you and they become your family. I still have a very good friend in Kentucky. From that time. I try to see him as often as possible.. We talk regularly on the phone.

After my service, I went to college on the GI bill of course. I got a bachelor's degree in mechanical engineering. I got married to my high school sweetheart who had seen me through my service and had two children, Wes and Ivey. I am now "Pops" to Magnolia and Jack. In 1989, I started my own company as a Mechanical Contractor in the Atlanta, Georgia area. I buried myself in my work and family, putting military and Vietnam completely behind me. I got on with my life. I now have experienced many things other people will never know. I am sure it has made me a better man.

I never talked to my wife, children, or family members about my deployment. But it was still there. It just didn't seem worth it to relive it, and I knew they would not understand that lifestyle... you just have to live it.

When I retired, I moved to Anderson, South Carolina. My wife bought me a hat with the 101st eagle on it. I was reluctant to wear it but eventually did put it on. I was approached by a couple of vets from the group Vets Helping Vets and was invited to a meeting. I declined for a while and finally gave in. I am glad I did because this group has shown me there is nothing wrong with being a Vietnam veteran.

Vets Helping Vets, especially the Monday night group, have shown me that it is OK to talk about those times. I enjoy the guys in this group as they understand the life of an infantry soldier. I have always been a proud American and now with the help of Vets Helping Vets, I am a proud American Veteran. Thank you, guys!

Gene Cromer

My name is Aubrey Eugene Cromer. I go by Gene. I was born in September of 1945 and reared on the Appleton Mill Village in the city limits of Anderson, South Carolina. My father worked in the mill his entire life. Some people called us lintheads from the cotton dust that accumulated on our clothes and hair from the poor exhaust systems of the mills. Like most, we were poor but did not know it. We called it working for a living.

Dad could not read or write. He never stayed in a motel or took a vacation. Around the time I was twelve, he did what so many others still do; he walked out on his wife and four kids.

By fourteen I was working at Pinson's Grocery Store on West Whitner Street making about three dollars for twelve hours. Then I worked for Hardy's Curb Market and Cooley's in the Homeland Park area. Mama had her problems, so I supported my two sisters and one brother the best I could. I was the one they came to with problems and I was the one who talked to their teachers at school. I kept the house and helped make sure they had food. I did not have a childhood and worked while going to school. Often, holding down two jobs, driving a school bus in the morning before school; and coming home after school to get ready to go to my grocery store job.

In 1963, I graduated from Crescent High School and went to work at Owens Corning Fiberglass. I married Carolyn Higginbotham in 1965 and soon received a letter from the U. S. Selective Service to report to Fort Jackson for my physical.

There I was told I was being drafted into the U. S. Army and to go home and get my affairs in order. I came home and talked to a buddy of mine, Robert McGaha. He and I went to an Air Force Recruiter. Because I had not took the official oath, I was allowed to raise my right hand and join the U. S. Air Force in 1966. We were to catch a commercial plane at Charlotte Douglas Airport then fly to Lackland Air Force Base in Texas. The recruiter said not to take extra clothes. We would be issued what we needed when we got there. Unfortunately, there was an airstrike going on and there we sat for three days. No change of clothes, just waiting. The recruiter booked us seats on a train, and we departed. It took us forty hours to reach our destination in Texas.

After basic at Lackland, I received orders to go to tech school in Amarillo, Texas to be a Supply Management Specialist. My wife, Carolyn, joined me in Amarillo and we rented a small apartment. Then I received orders to go to Warner Robbins Air Force Base in Georgia. In January 1968, I received orders for Da Nang, Vietnam. My job was to monitor the aircraft such as the F4s and F105s that were grounded due to mechanical problems. As a Supply Specialist, I would order the parts needed to get them back in the air. Carolyn wrote me every day while I was in Vietnam. Often, I would write her back, and put the time and date on the backside of the envelope. The 6 o'clock news frightened her with tragedy after tragedy from Da Nang. She could check the time and date of my letter and compare the details from the anchorman and hopefully I was writing after the fact; letting her know I was still alive.

While in Da Nang, our base was in an area they called 'rocket alley' because we were constantly bombarded with rocket attacks. Every day, we heard the siren, a warning to seek shelter in a bunker. The guards posted in towers around the perimeters announced incoming. Oh, but we knew they were coming for we heard the whistling sound of the whining rockets. Many times, it was best to stop running and hit the ground. You were safer lying still unless it was a direct hit. My buddy, Clifford Lefler, took a direct mortar round and was killed.

I received news the building I had worked in was hit, and all three people I worked with was killed. Those are the close calls that haunt you and leave you sad for the lives lost. Yet, coming home we were told not to wear our uniforms because the hippies were protesting, throwing rocks, calling us names such as 'baby killers,' and spitting on returning soldiers. Those disrespectful cowards could not see for the lies the media spread. We were young people like them who did not ask to be tangled in the Vietnam War. What we experienced and saw would impact us for the rest of our lives. I know one thing, we were patriotic, hardworking Americans who did not have time to protest or organize sit-ins.

I rotated out after a year, and in January 1969, I was assigned to the Charleston Air Force Base in South Carolina. I remained in Charleston until I was released from military service in July of 1970. Returning home, I became a father in August of 1970. The very next day after my son Brian was born, I became a fulltime student at Anderson College (University) and worked weekends at Owens Corning. The next August after graduating, I enrolled at Erskine College, Due West, South Carolina. After a full load of classes, I graduated in August 1972 with a degree in Business Administration. Our second son, Kevin, was born in 1972.

There has never been a time when I have not worked. I worked for Cochran Realty selling residential homes as sales manager. In 1976, a friend Larry Stone and I created a business, Cromer and Stone, building apartment homes, developing subdivisions, and commercial buildings in South Carolina and North Carolina. We went on to build doctor's offices, restaurants, three large spas, and over five hundred houses. Eventually, I went out on my own (Cromer Company) in residential investments and building. I have two sons. Kevin finished the University of South Carolina. Brian finished Furman University where he double majored and received two diplomas. Then he went to Syracuse University in New York and received his master's. From there, he went to Northwestern University in Chicago where he received his Doctor of Law. He finished up with a master's in divinity at Columbia Theological College in Georgia. Our two granddaughters, Addie and Lila, finished Carolina. One is in banking and the other works in a non-profit organization. Our grandson Field graduated high school this year and already has his pilot license. He starts classes at the University of South Carolina in the fall. His ultimate plan is to be a commercial pilot.

Our children have strong work ethics. Our grandson has his own pressure washing business. He is learning that good old fashion hard work is still the key to success.

Combine that with an education and opportunities are endless. It helps level the playing field.

Civilians do not understand that those who served were forever changed. I do not think I even understood that coming home, going straight to the work force, school and civilian life. As I got older, I saw it so much clearer and understood my habit like making sure there is a clear path for an exit if one is needed. Sudden noise startles me, even at a military funeral where I know there will be a gun salute. Flashbacks surprise me and others when I believe to be back in Da Nang. I dare not trust my eyes or thoughts.

Jesse Taylor invited me to a Vets Helping Vets Anderson meeting. I was wearing a hat in the local Lowes Home Store, and he recognized me as a veteran. I visited when there were under thirty people attending. Gradually the membership grew. I look forward to when we can have our own place and not have to move again. The key to the future of VHVA will be the young veterans from more recent conflicts. Right now, we are an aging group of veterans paving the way to ensure these young veterans will have a place to meet and share the camaraderie we enjoy. Hopefully, they find healing and understanding from like-minded veterans.

William Dawson Crowe

William Dawson Crowe, better known as "Bill," was born on January 25, 1929. He served 23 years in the Air Force, retiring as Senior Master Sergeant, E-8. Bill was born on a mill village at #4 Dunean Drive in Greenville, South Carolina. His father was a barber for the mill company store, paid four dollars a month rent for the house they lived in, and had to give one half of his earnings back to the mill. Haircuts were ten cents and a shave fifteen cents—hence the saying, "Shave and a haircut two bits."

Bill's military story began in 1950 when he and two buddies went to Anderson Draft Board to talk about opportunities. They knew they were about to get drafted into the Army and wanted to pick their branch of service. The recruiter told them a stack of draft letters was indeed going out the next day. They all felt sure they would receive one. The recruiter said the Navy currently was not accepting applicants, but the Air Force was. They discussed their options and left. Bill went back alone the next day and enlisted in the Air Force.

He was sent to Lackland Air Force Base in San Antonio, Texas, for basic training on August 22, 1950. Bill thought one of the hardest things about basic training was the food which did not include simple things he enjoyed at home such as pinto beans and cornbread. Plus, he missed his family.

They also had a mean, bossy Drill Instructor who harassed them constantly. During basic training, the airmen were restricted to the barracks. Bill's crew of friends talked one of them into sneaking out to the BX to get candy for all of them. On his way back to the barracks, he was caught red-handed. The DI asked him what he had in the sack, to which he honestly replied, "candy."

"Oh, so you want some candy, do you? Then eat all of it –the whole bag." Bill's friend did as ordered, whereupon he promptly puked, then had to clean it all up. They never tried that again.

The airmen's favorite song was the country western "Oh, how I wanna go home" by Bobby Bare.

Bill's first assignment was to serve as an MP, Military Police, at McCord Air Force Base, Tacoma, Washington. It was a very cold climate. Once, when Bill came home to the barracks after serving guard duty four hours in a cold rain, a sergeant was there asking for volunteers for Food Services. Bill was the first to volunteer. He was soon sent to the Cook and Bakers School at Ft. Louis, Washington and then to a dining hall at McCord.

The dining hall workers were at first a segregated group of men. Black airmen were all in one squadron and ate in this dining hall. They were gradually integrated, among the first in the military. At the beginning of Bill's time, there might be one shift of white airmen and two of black airmen, Then, little-by-little, as workers were sick or any vacancies occurred, the crew began to be mixed. Critics said, "That will ruin the military," but the complete opposite turned out to be true, because every man, black or white, just wanted to be the best.

A guy named Ford from New York in the Food Services outfit nicknamed Bill, "Ernie," because he thought Bill's Southern accent sounded like Tennessee Ernie Ford. He called the Southern people "hayseeds." Bill and his buddies had a few tricks up their sleeve to exact a little bit of payback from him. He slept with his mouth open. The young airmen poured an entire bottle of pancake syrup down his throat while he slept. He drank it all. When he awakened, he told the other men that he dreamed he and his dad robbed the beehive. He said the dream was so real, he still had a real sweet taste in his mouth. When he was sleeping on his stomach with his arm hanging off the bed, the airmen put that arm in a warm bucket of water. That trick caused a wet bed.

They tried several pranks, such as "short sheeting," which folds and arranges the sheet in such a way that anyone getting into the bed will be unable to stretch their legs out beyond the middle of the bed. Bill and his friends also started a campaign designed to stir the imagination and frighten him. Whenever he was about to fall asleep, they would hoarsely whisper, "They are watching you." The young men finally did it any time they walked by him, and in such frightful whispers that it worked and scared him plenty.

Then Bill was sent overseas by plane, where he did a tour of duty in Korea and then Viet Nam. Bill said the tours were so different. In Korea he had a front line, the 38th Parallel. Beyond that boundary was the enemy. In Viet Nam, he never knew where the battle would be or who the enemy was. Some of the enemies, unbeknownst to the military, worked on the base. A few even brought explosives into the dining hall.

On Bill's first night in Viet Nam, he was sleeping against the wall in double-decker bunks. A 90MM rocket hit beside the barracks, but got stuck in the wet, muddy side of the wall and did not explode. During the rainy season, the whole world of Viet Nam was wet and muddy—no escape from it. Thankfully, no one was injured by the rocket, but it was terrifying.

Another troubling thing: the hospital mortuary was near the dining hall. Airmen would know when bodies came in because of the helicopters landing, and they could hear awful discussions about processing the dead and see terrible things. A sixteen-member team handled the duties after helicopters delivered the dead young men. Bill and a Lieutenant or Captain together took possession of the deceased's personal belongings, and they put the items in a pouch attached to the casket.

The one good thing Bill had going for him was a military buddy with a Hawaiian girlfriend who worked typing specs for AT&T. She could somehow rig them up to make calls to folks at home. The conversations went something like this:

"Hello, over."

How are the girls, over?

I love you, over."

But those calls were a God send.

Bill was to ship out from Viet Nam for home on August 22, 1967. On August 10ⁿ, 1967, Bill received word from the

60

Red Cross that his wife Jeral was having major surgery. Bill's superior advised him to try to get home. Even though the surgery was not life threatening, it was serious. Bill was able to get on a cargo plane with seven webbed seats, all taken. In the cargo bay, seven coffins carried bodies back to the states. In flight, the plane took a direct hit, which made a hole in the cargo bay. They dropped the cargo ramp over the hole. They landed in Thailand and changed planes, reloading the coffins in the process.

Bill arrived at Dover, Delaware, and took a civilian plane back home to Lackland Air Force Base in Texas. A friend picked him up at the airport and carried him to the hospital, where Bill got to speak briefly to Jeral and squeeze her hand as she was being transported to surgery. Bill was then feeling dizzy and almost passed out. A nurse asked when was the last time he had eaten. He had been traveling for twenty-seven hours straight and had eaten nothing. The nurse remedied that situation with a tray of food, and Bill felt much better.

Bill agrees that stories about war being "hell" are all true. Many of his own stories are so graphic and horrible, Bill would not talk about them for years. Bill recently became acquainted with lines from a Wendell Berry book which makes the point that dealing with war memories is impossible because we have insufficient words to describe its horror: The word, "they" in the quote refers to military men who saw combat.

"And they said not a word. They stood among us like monuments without inscriptions. They said nothing or said little because we barely have a language for what they knew, and they could not bear the pain of talking of their knowledge in even so poor a language as we have."

When he returned to civilian life, he had nightmares and suffered from PTSD. Bill finally concluded that what helped him most in dealing with PTSD was to find a good listener to talk with about his experiences. After talking with several counselors, that is what they all decided. Bill should find trusting friends or associates who didn't try to offer advice but were compassionate listeners.

Bill's nightmares resumed when he was around death. When Bill's Father and then later Jeral's Father both were dying and Bill was dealing with those issues, his nightmares resumed. When a neighbor's husband died, she asked Bill to come over to help, which he did. His nightmares resumed. Bill learned a new trauma can sometimes wipe out a previous trauma, but there is still a trauma in the mix. So, Bill decided that he would no longer go to funerals or visitations or wakes, and he has conquered the nightmares with God's help. He is reminded of the Wendell Berry quote in his "Hannah Coulter" book: "You can't give yourself over to love for a soldier without giving yourself to his suffering in war." PTSD affects many servicemen, but it also affects their family. Bill is extremely thankful for his wife Jeral's support and support from his church.

The thing most positive about his military career is that he learned to have much more confidence in himself and stand up for what is right. Once, while in the military, he and a fellow airman were talking to the base Commander, who was asking a lot of questions. To one of his questions Bill replied, "No Sir, that is not correct," and proceeded to tell him what was correct. Bill's fellow employee told him later, "Bill, you need to be more careful how you speak." Bill reminded him that the Commander thanked him and said he appreciated his honesty and needed to hear it. That really helped build Bill's confidence.

Bill moved fourteen times during his military service. He lived in San Antonio, Texas; Tacoma, Washington; Korea; Panama City, Florida, the outskirts of London, England. From England, he moved back to San Antonio, Texas, where he was reminded that the worsted wools from England would not do for the San Antonio climate.

During his career, Bill earned three Air Force Commendation medals, four Good Conduct medals and numerous Service Medals. He never had a "good luck charm," but depended on common sense and the care of his Savior, no matter where he lived.

When he retired from the service, he was glad to shed the uniform, especially the hat. Bill never liked wearing a hat, and he did not like the military haircut. Once home, his wife Jeral started cutting his hair and did so for a while. He says he cannot discard some military habits such as folding his socks just so, in fact all his clothes just so.

When one meets Bill today, one sees a military bearing, a strong handshake, a quick smile, a twinkle in his eyes, and usually a joke on his lips. He speaks highly of the local Veterans Administration. While discussing a recent appointment there, he talks about a hefty nurse taking his vitals, checking his weight, and scanning his medical records. She put hands on hips and sassily asked, "Mr. Crowe, how old are you?" When he answered, "ninety-four," she replied, "Mr. Crowe you are a miracle."

Interviewed and written by: Patricia Jones Wood, Foothills Writers Guild

David Davis

My name is David Lee Davis, nicknamed big D for I did bodybuilding. I grew up in Georgetown Ohio, Chicago Illinois, and Columbus Ohio. I carried newspapers, worked in food service, and grocery stores during these times in my life. A highlight of my time in Chicago was when I was in the seventh grade, I was selected to represent the Chicago Milk Foundation for public schools with the United States Secretary of Agriculture, Ezra Taft Benson.

On February 28, 1961, I entered the US Air Force before graduation. I was living in Columbus Ohio at the time where I graduated from North High School. I joined the military because I was not accepted at the Air Force Military Academy. I was into electronics, so I chose the Air Force as my branch of service and served during the Vietnam era.

After graduation I took my basic training at Lackland Air Force Base in Texas. 3724th Squadron, Flight 244. One funny moment in boot camp was when one of the airmen was caught fishing on the parade grounds. A Sergeant asked him what he was fishing for, and he said he was fishing for a discharge. The Sergeant told him if he caught one, he would go fishing with him. Some things I remember about adapting to a military life: doing what you are told to do, making your bed first, and how to KP the right way.

I went to electronic school in Biloxi Mississippi and schooled in Heavy Ground Radio Repair and Minuteman missile guidance systems. My assignments included Lockbourne Air Force Base Columbus Ohio, Strategic Air

Command 301st Bomb Wing, 376th Air Refueling Squadron, 801st Headquarters Squadron, and I received orders to Francis E Warren Air Force Base, Cheyenne, Wyoming, 90th Missile Wing.

The things I remember most about my deployment was during the Cuban missile crisis. I was deployed to Homestead Air Force Base, Homestead, Florida to back up heavy ground radio communication between the Air Force and the Navy. On returning to Lockbourne, my duty changed to escort duty for the 801st Headquarters Operation and distribution of payroll.

During my time in the Air Force, I learned how to adapt quickly and to support my mission. I was awarded the four-year ribbon and expert in small arms. Someone I remember fondly is Larry Puffinbarger. Larry and I loved to go to the drag races at Dragway 42, in West Salem, Ohio when we were on leave. Some fun things we did during deployment in Cheyenne were horseback riding, playing softball and football.

We did some humorous things like putting lighter fluid in our mouth and blowing it out towards a lit match and yelling "Fire, Fire!" at 3 o'clock in the morning. We would go to a truck stop, order chili and distract one guy. Then load his chili up with hot pepper seeds.

During that time, I was stationed at Lockbourne Air Force Base, I was escort for President John F. Kennedy, Vice President Lyndon B. Johnson, General Curtis LeMay, Commander of Strategic Air Command (SAC), actor and Brigadier General Jimmy Stewart. I escorted baseball players Willie Mays, Roger Maris and Mickey Mantle, and football's

Green Bay Packers, Paul Horning, also astronaut John Glenn. There were many others but memories fade with time.

I did not see combat due to working with the Minutemen Missiles. My orders finally came through for Francis E. Warren Air Force Base in Cheyenne Wyoming where I was assigned to the 90th Missile Wing. I worked on the Minuteman One from June 1963 to February 1965, installing guidance systems and was discharged from the military on February 5, 1965. They asked me to extend my time and go to Vietnam as an advisor, but I declined.

My first few months out of the service went well. I went to spend time on my grandmother's farm in Georgetown, Ohio and did some odd jobs for about eight months. My civilian life began in Columbus, Ohio when I applied to Franklin Engineering Ltd., as a draft person working on interstate highways. Thus began my forty plus years in Civil Engineering.

My schooling included Ohio State University, Florida State University, Florida University and Manatee Community College. My jobs during my forty plus years included: Highway Design, Land Surveyor and designing subdivisions for the first ten-year period. For the next ten years, I was Street Superintendent for the city of Sidney, Ohio. During the next six years, I designed ceramic kilns for Harrop Services all over the world. My final job was in Manatee County, Florida as a Traffic Engineer to computerize the traffic signal system for the county.

I received recognition by being published in Who's Who International in Public Safety 2000-2002. I retired at age sixty-two after fourteen years with Manatee County, Florida. The word respect magnifies my life following my service. I wish all civilians had to enlist in the service to obtain structure in their life. They would know what the true meaning is to serve your country before condemning your country. Habits I like following, from my time in the service, is making my bed every morning and supporting my fellow veterans.

I wrote about my memories that included my time in the Air Force and gave copies to my four daughters from my previous marriages. I have now been married for twenty-three years to Penny Davis. We have a blended family of eight children and eighteen grandchildren.

Throughout my life we have enjoyed camping, fishing, hunting, and playing in city league softball teams. I collect U.S. stamps and coins and Murano glass from Italy. We are Ohio State University football fans and belong to a club in Greenville with over a thousand members. We are members of Central Presbyterian Church and are both church Elders. My organizations are: 32-degree Mason; Lodge 31; Scottish Rite Valley of Tampa Florida; American Legion, Bradenton Florida; and Elks Lodge; and Vets Helping Vets, Anderson, South Carolina.

My wife Penny and I have traveled all over the world including China, Ireland, Greece, Italy, Germany, Australia, and fifteen cruises in the last twenty-three years. It has been a great journey the last 81 years. Being a member of Vets Helping Vets has been inspiring; experiencing time with the family of those who have served our country and share a common bond.

John Firneno

My name is John Paul Firneno. Co-workers gave me the nickname of Greywolf because of my obvious grey hair. I enlisted and took the oath September 28, 1970, when was living on the south side of Chicago, Illinois. The Vietnam war was on, and I did not want to wait to get drafted, There was not really anything at home to keep me there. I went to basic training at Lackland Air Force Base, San Antonio, Texas. The first two years I served in a Red Horse unit as a Combat Engineer. The Red Horse is what the Air force called their combat construction team. The second two years I crossed trained as a combat medic. I was stationed at Nellis Air Force Base, Nevada; Luke Air Force Base, Arizona; and in Germany.

I chose the Air Force because I wanted to become a jet engine mechanic, but that never happened. My Advanced Individual Training (AIT) was on-the-job-training (OJT) as a Engineer/Carpenter Specialist. I rarely had a hammer in my hand, we were usually digging trenches. We did very little carpenter work.

We rarely had time to find anything funny during Basic Training, they were pushing people through so fast to replenish the troops. I adapted to military life but the problems I had come a little later when I realized that though some had more stripes they actually did not know what they were doing half the time. This caused me to feel a little jaded, but I figured out how to do things for myself. I developed a

69

good rapport with other sergeants and the officers who often came to me to get their questions answered.

While stationed in Germany, I had a situation where the officer and I did not see eye-to-eye about things. We were working on revetments for our fighter jets. Revetments are barrier walls made of concrete for reinforcement to protect the jet from incoming artillery if the enemy tries to skip a bomb into the hangar. It would hit the wall first. The wall was four feet wide, but it could be twenty-four feet high. They decided to put lights on the top and have us work on the wall at night. They placed lights around the bottom and pointed them up in our direction, but they did not illuminate the whole twenty-four feet. One of our guys almost fell off as we were walking the top to step onto the crane bucket to take us back down. I was right behind him and grabbed him by his collar to pull him back up.

I told my NCOIC at dinner what happened and that we were not going back out to work in the dark, he replied that we would. I told him I would not work up there in the darkness unless he was willing to go up there in the dark to work. I did not go back out. The NCOIC took the rest of the men back out that night and realized what I was talking about. They all came back in quickly. I was still in trouble, at least for a while.

While working as an engineer, building a structure, one of the young guys ask us how we were going to lift the big metal trusses up to the top. We send him looking for a skyhook. He asked us what a skyhook is, and we tell him to go to the back of the trailer and he would find it in a blue box with white clouds. He comes back about twenty minutes later without a skyhook, and we are laughing. The guy realizes there was no such thing as a skyhook.

When I came back to Nellis AFB for a combat medic, they did not have a place for me. I was placed in the Labor and Delivery Maternity Ward where I met my future wife, Linda. She was an officer and worked there as a nurse. I got out of the Air Force in April 1974 after marrying Linda. We have been married over fifty years. My plan had been to stay in for twenty years but once I saw the way certain things were back in the states, I was glad I got out.

The military taught me to be my own boss. I became very self-sufficient. I believe the youth of today would benefit by going into the military, but I know not everyone is cut out for that. Our son joined the military. There were no wars going on and he was undecided about college or career choses. He ended up making a heck of a career out of it as an Army Combat Medic. My grandson is a drone operator in the U. S. Army. The military gives you a lot of opportunities and on-the-job training with skills to use throughout life.

Vets Helping Vets Anderson invest their skills to help other veterans. They work towards a common goal. It is a place where veterans can relate with others who have had the same experiences. They know how you feel because they have been there and done that.

Linda Firneno

I am Linda Marie Courtet Firneno, and I enlisted in May 19, 1972. A couple of months before, a friend and I who lived in Maryland went to the Andrews Air Force Base to talk to a recruiter. I wanted to go into the United States Army because both my parents had served during WWII.

My dad was an Sergeant in the U.S. Army and was stationed at Pearl Harbor on December 7, 1941. He was coming back from his barracks when the Japanese planes flew overhead to bomb Pearl Harbor. He was in service for four years and received three Purple Hearts, the Bronze Medal with a Silver Star. He never talk about that, so we never knew what happened. I got the information later when I was looking up genealogy material and found out what he had done. My mom was an officer. She was an Army nurse and felt that this was her calling because her brothers and others were serving. Mom went in towards the end of WWII.

She ended up getting hepatitis and was sent back to the states. Interestingly enough the plane she was supposed to be going on Went down in the South Pacific. Fortunately, when she had got sicker, she was placed on a flight that was leaving sooner. Someone called my grandmother to tell her my mom had died on the plane that went down. Then my mom wrote my grandmother telling her she had been sick, my grandmother passed out thinking she was reading a letter from a ghost.

She went to upstate New York. My dad was from New Jersey and came up to visit her when he got out. They got married and had five children. My mother worked as a nurse and retired when she was sixty-five. She lived to be ninety-five years old. When she passed she was buried at Arlington National Cemetery in Arlington, Virginia with full military honors.

I was a registered nurse and had a three year diploma. The Army and the Navy would not let me go in as an officer because they had their own schools. I went in as a First Lieutenant not a Second Lieutenant with the Air Force because of all my working experience since I had been out of nursing school.

I went to basic training at Sheppard Air Force Base. This was interesting because we only had two weeks training that included running a mile. We got up 8:00 o'clock in the morning and other kind of odd things. Then I got sent to Nellis Air Force Base in Nevada. The Air Force gives you a dream sheet and I had signed up to be a flight nurse out of Vietnam and I ended up at Nellis Air Force Base in Las Vegas on the maternity ward. It was a good experience because that is where I met my husband John. With me as an officer and John as a NCO, we knew there would be trouble mixing service with marriage. Soon I got orders to the Philippines, and he got orders to Korea. I told my commanding officer that we do not want to be separated. She said, "Well at least you're in the same area." I said, "5000 miles apart." She reminded me we would have a thirty day leave.

We made the decision to leave the military and did not reenlist. We have been married for fifty years and working in the maternity ward was a good practice for future parents of three children. We moved to New Jersey and eventually out to Salt Lake, Utah. We lost a son when he was sixteen. Our daughter lives in Louisiana and works at Ochsner Medical Center. Our other son joined the military after of high School. We have five grandchildren.

Once when my son was stationed in Haiti, He was doing rounds at night when at 2:00 o'clock in the morning there was a Haitian lady on the side of the road In a stalled vehicle. He stopped to help her and delivered a baby boy. The story was carried on all news channels because President Clinton, Past President Carter and General Colin Powell were there because it was the end of the conflict with Haiti. I remember the speech: "As his comrades clustered around him with flashlights, Private First Class John Paul Firneno delivered a seven pound four ounce baby boy and she named him after him, John Paul."

I would recommend the military to any young person searching for their niche in life. The military would be a great start. You can serve your country, learn job skills, and attend college for free. I went back to the University of Utah and received my bachelors in psychology. I went into psychology as a nurse counselor and at fifty-five years old I got my License Professional Counselor with a masters in psychology. I took care of troubled teenagers and their families for thirty-five years.

My advice to the youth of today is you never know what your life is going to bring. I never knew I would end up in South Carolina. Take the opportunities that you are given.

If you are really struggling, talk to somebody because there is somebody out there who can understand your experiences.

Because I never got to serve anywhere other than labor and delivery at Nellis Air Force Base, I did not feel like I really served. Accompanying my son who was asked to speak at a Veteran's Day at school, I was sitting next to somebody who was a POW. I shared with him my feelings of not serving. He said, "Oh no, don't say that. We were so glad that there were people back home taking care of our families." That was the first time I ever felt there was a true reason for my service. I share this advice to men and women who may feel as I did. They need to tell their story because everybody plays a part.

Vets Helping Vets Anderson is a great place to start. They are doing a great job with those who need help. It is easier to talk to someone who knows what you are talking about.

Norm Garrett

My name is Norman P. Garrett. Following the launch of the TV show "Cheers" it's just Norm. I got married to my high school sweetheart in 1974. By 1975, we had hit rock bottom. I enlisted in the U. S. Navy to earn the GI Bill so I could finish college. I ultimately retired from the US Army in 2014.

I enlisted in the US Naval Reserve February 5, 1976, in the delayed entry program. The morning of February 23, 1976, my recruiter took me and a couple of other inductees to Military In Processing (MIPs) at Fort Jackson, Columbia, South Carolina. Late that afternoon, we were bussed to the Columbia Airport for our flight to Orlando, Florida to start basic training.

It was my first trip in a plane, and it was a short flight. We were herded on a bus well after midnight at the airport and taken to Recruit Training Center (RTC) Orlando. When we arrived, the yelling started, and we were herded off the bus. Each recruit fell in on a tile with their personal belongings. We were ordered to dump everything we had on the tile at our feet. Angry men swarmed over us and picked through our belongings.

Anything that could be used as a weapon was taken away including my razor blades and the glass in the picture frame holding the photo of my wife. They also took my daily vitamins, aspirin, and anything they did not like. They also pointed to the amnesty barrel yelling if you have any drugs this is your last chance, you will be drug tested in the morning.

Somewhere in all this we were formed up and marched

to a barracks known as the Recruit Indoctrination Facility (RIF). I think I spent two days there. I know it was a whirlwind. Shave off your beard and sideburns, tomorrow you will get a haircut. We ran our first physical test, a mile and half run in whatever civilian clothes we had. We marched to the clothing issue and were issued clothing to the shouts of what size do you wear? Sign this paper. NO, NO, NO, stencil your name here! Your name must be visible on your shirt and pants. You will not wear any uniform part belonging to your neighbor.

Reveille was at 0430 to the sound of clanging trash cans. UP, UP, UP, get out of that rack and get dressed. One lasting impression was never wear new clothes, always wash them first. All the new recruits smelled like RIF, the smell of Moth Balls. You wore tennis shoes not our boon dockers until you were formed up into a company. All our other uniforms were sent to the laundry.

I was lucky, I only remember being in RIF for two days. You stayed in RIF until there were enough guys to form a company. You wanted out as soon as possible; basic training did not officially start until you were in a company. I was placed in Company 250 and marched off to our new barracks. Our Company Commander was Radioman (RM) First Class Trujillo. Petty Officer (PO) Trujillo was a Native American. We later adopted the name Trujillo's Tribe for our company flag. We were his first company.

The first days were a blur. I remember the swim test. It was February in Orlando, and we were marched over to an outside pool. Jump in and tread water. If you made the allotted time you stayed with the company to finish training. There were three "special" companies at basic; the Rocks, guys who failed the swim test; the Wrecks, guys who failed the run, and Special Ed, guys with academic problems. You were held in the special companies until you could swim, run, or pass whatever test they gave. As a side note, the guys in the Special Ed company could march rings around everyone else. They had a swagger when they marched. This time was in addition to basic training.

I enlisted at the ripe old age of 21 and was made a squad leader day one in training. I do not remember how many guys were in my squad; I have no idea how many were in my company. We lived in an open bay barracks with rifle racks running down the center. Each recruit was assigned a piece, a 1903 Springfield, to be his very own. We spent a LOT of time polishing our pieces and learning how to march with them. Our racks, upper and lower were on either side of the rifle racks. Our lockers were stacked two high on the end. Each locker had two open boxes which held our clothing folded in regulation style.

We had one locking drawer for our valuables and stuff that did not look good on display. Each locker had a regulation pad lock with the key attached to our dog tags, which never left our necks. The lockers were small, but they taught us how to live on a ship with minimal storage space. Sometime late in our second week I was asked if I would be the Recruit Chief Petty Officer (RCPO). His job was to get the troops to their appointed station throughout the day and to maintain military discipline at all times.

Since I was asked, I declined the honor. I was told by everybody I knew with any military experience to maintain a low profile. After the Assistant Company Commander (ACC), a very salty Seaman Apprentice (E-2) who had just graduated from basic himself finished chewing my rear end off, I happily agreed to the honor of being the RCPO. I moved up to the front of the barracks and was taught how to march.

I was later told they tried a couple of other guys in the position. They could march great but had a problem with commands and scheduling. I was a baby NUC, nuclear field candidate. I had the basics in operating the company or at least was a very quick study, but I walked and marched like a stiff white boy. I literally had to be taught how to swing my arms when I marched. I was also the butt of many jokes by the ACC and CC. What is lower than whale poop at the bottom of the ocean? A NUC! What is drift'er than bean soup, a NUC! The jokes kept coming.

Navy basic training consisted of daily calisthenics for physical training. I do not remember running much but we marched everywhere we went as a company. We spent a lot of time in the classroom learning all about shipboard life. We learned firefighting; Mr. RCPO you will be the first man into the burning building as nozzleman on hose one, your Yeoman will have the spray hose to keep you protected. I hope you did not make him mad today. We did gasmask training in the gas chamber. Mr. RCPO you will be the first one in and the last one out; breathe deep for full enjoyment.

We had first aid training, inspections, time on the ship mockup, small arms training with 1911 pistols, and everything you can think of to prepare us for life on a Navy ship. I will never forget the mistakes. I marched the company on the grass, Mr. RCPO you just marched your company into the water and drowned them. When we get back to the barracks give me 20, 30, or 50 pushups depending on the week of training and how the CC felt. Any infractions brought extra physical training.

We came back into the barracks early in training and found the place completely trashed. Everything we owned that was not locked up was in one corner of the building. Three or four of us had lockers that survived. We were ordered into the lounge, facing away from the window and were allowed to smoke and joke. The Corpsman sat with us. As soon as a couple of the guys went down, they called the Corpsman out and the lesson was complete. We worked overtime from top down to ensure ALL lockers were up to standard at all times.

I did something stupid on the company street one day. When we got back to the barracks and the company staff, RCPO, Platoon Leaders, Squad Leaders, and Yeoman, were ordered out in front of the barracks office in raincoats. We performed physical training (PT) until somebody got sick and then were allowed to fallout. When I left Basic I was in very good shape and had very strong arms. I did a LOT of pushups.

One of the highlights of basic training were the shots. They used the air propelled shot guns on us. We marched to medical, stripped off our shirts, tied them around out waist, and walked through the gauntlet. The corpsman stood on both sides with the guns; they cleaned our arm and shot us. If you moved, you got cut, more than one arm in the line was bleeding.

I only remember one bad shot. We got it late in the day and marched back to the barracks where we took it easy. Later that evening a number of guys were sick, and the Corpsmen came to visit. Week six was service week. Everyone was given a support assignment. A lot of guys ended up in the galley doing KP. Some did grounds work. I was assigned as RCPO of the brig. The "brig" was a small barracks with a desk and a couple of racks. We marched the "prisoners" to chow or anywhere they needed to be. We were given a deserter to watch, his dad talked him into turning himself in so he could quite running. He was to be held long enough to be processed out of the Navy on a bad conduct discharge. He did not like the hospitality; he bolted after two days. All we could do was watch him run; we had no training or authority to stop him. After service week we were rewarded. We made an exchange run, bought candy, cookies, and sodas and had a picnic.

We also finished our screening for rate assignments. In the Navy everyone has a rating or career group. E-1 through E-3 are strikers. A striker prepares for a rate through on-the-job training in the fleet, attending a school, or has been selected for the rate. When one makes E-4 they become a Petty Officer in a particular rating. This is very confusing unless you are a sailor. When I enlisted, I had been guaranteed the Nuclear Field. As such, I signed up for 6 years. I entered basic training as a recruit like everyone else but when I graduated, I was an E-3.

The Nuclear Field had four ratings, Machinist Mate (MM), Electricians Mate (EM), Interior Communications Specialist (IC), and Electronics Technician (ET). The Navy always selected your rating based on the needs of the Navy. I wanted MM and was selected for this rate. I had a high mechanical aptitude, and the Navy needed more MM's than the other rates. When I graduated from basic, I had the three red stripes of an E-3 Engineering Rating on my sleeve.

Graduation finally arrived and we were minted as new sailors. As a bonus at the end of basic training, I was selected as the Outstanding Recruit from my Company. I left basic training as an E-3 MM striker heading to Machinist Mate "A" School. The school was located in the beautiful Great Lakes Naval Training Command. I still maintain Great Lakes is the arm pit of the United States. I have Army friends tell me that Fort Polk has that honor, but I beg to differ.

I was transported to Charleston, South Carolina for two weeks leave before I had to report for duty. I went car shopping and found a large, used, four-door Chrysler product to purchase. My Dad surprised me and picked up the tab. I loaded up my wife Anita, most of what we owned except a few beat-up pieces of furniture and drove to Illinois.

Navy housing helped us find a wonderful place in Waukegan. It was a very old house that had been subdivided into three apartments. We got a furnished apartment on the second floor accessed by a steep stairway added to the side of the house. The sofa in the "living" room had a beer can for one leg. The walls were extremely colorful, but it had the basics, so we camped out for a couple of months.

My "A" School was self-paced. I finished the "classroom" portion in less than five days. I spent a couple of days helping out students who had problems and helping out the foreign students. We were awash in Middle Eastern sailors trying to learn the basics so they could crew a couple of destroyers we gave them. This was a hard spot for us. They were paid well by their country and apparently the US Government also supplemented their salary. They did much better than the average American sailor. It took a couple of weeks to get through the watch standing portion, they needed to get other sailors out of school and out to sea.

The highlights of Great Lakes included getting written up for walking on the grass, a heinous crime which cost me a Saturday mornings extra duty. Since I was a "brown bagger" and lived off base, I did evening duty as Shore Patrol (SP) cruising the base and the enlisted men's club. We were paired up, issued SP arm bands and night sticks. We were told to only poke never to hit with the stick, and we were off to police the base. Thankfully, no fights broke out when I had the duty.

At the end of "A" School, I signed my two year extension and was promoted to Machinist Mate Third Class (MM3). I was an E-4 under six months obligated for six-years' service. I was in the nuclear pipeline and my next school did not start for a couple of months. I was given the option to go to an old World War II cruiser in Charleston, SC or stay as a Learning Supervisor Assistant (LSA) in MM "A" School. I picked LSA so I did not have to move again. We stayed at the Great Lakes through the summer into late fall.

Entertainment at Great Lakes consisted of loading up

the land yacht with Anita and a bunch of Navy buddies and running up to Kenosha, Wisconsin for the drag races. We ate out at A&W Root Bear and visited the EM club at both Great Lakes and Fort Sheridan (Fort Shaky). The couple that lived behind us were Army, so they showed us around Fort Shaky. We also ran down to Chicago a couple of times. We ate real deep dish pizza down in the loop and visited the museums. I also remember trying to drive down to see a sailing ship on the Lakes and spending four hours in bumper to bumper traffic on a Sunday afternoon. I learned then to stay out of big cities. My time was finally up and as we left Great Lakes the first snowflakes started hitting the ground. Next Stop was Orlando, Florida.

We drove to Charleston for a couple of days leave and then to Orlando to start the next phase. I had to report for the long prep school, I needed to get my math up to speed. We rented a nice house just outside the base and shared it with another Navy couple. We should have rented an apartment like everyone else. Sharing a house was a learning experience; I never did that again.

Preschool was six weeks long and concentrated on math. Nuclear Power School was six months long, eight hours a day. We started with twelve sections with about thirty students in each section. We were grouped by our preschool scores and by rate. I was appointed Section Leader for Section 8, all Machinist Mates. There was at least one section of electrical types in Section one through seven.

Nuclear Power school was at a minimum an Associate of Science degree in Nuclear Engineering Technology crammed into six months. For eight hours a day we studied math, physics, electrical theory, chemistry, thermodynamics, materials, the basics of radioactivity, and reactor theory. As an MM, we were taught pumps, valves, and other mechanical basics. By the third month the lower seven sections looked like a ghost town.

The attrition rate was high. Guys failed due to academics, they just could not handle everything thrown at them or they gave up. Some took a bust to E-3 for a minor offence and went to sea. Guys that failed out trying were given good follow on assignments. A lot of guys got gas turbine school or went to submarine school. The guys who gave up got a quick reassignment to the fleet on any ship that needed a body. The stress level was very high; everyone was required to work hard. Everyone in power school was challenged.

Following Nuclear Power School, I completed prototype training and Engineering Laboratory Technician (ELT) school at Naval Prototype Training Unit (NPTU) Idaho Falls in April 1978. "Prototype" was six months training in reactor operations. I was assigned to the S5G submarine prototype. The Navy built the prototypes to test reactor and shipboard concepts then used the equipment to train nukes. I did extremely well at prototype. I was guaranteed an additional school or possibly a position on staff, two more years on shore. I wanted to go to welding school but was talked into applying for both welding school and ELT school. I should have known better; I was assigned to ELT school.

I had been promoted to MM2 during prototype and I

was looking forward to my first assignment. I was gung-ho. I was selected to be an ELT staff instructor after I was given orders to a boat. I turned down instructor duty because I had orders to the U.S.S. Francis Scott Key SSBN-657 Blue in Charleston, South Carolina. One of my ELT instructors had served on the Key and assured me it was a great boat. The SSBN submarines had two complete crews. One crew took the submarine to sea and the other crew had off-crew. Off-crew consisted of about 3 weeks off with no duties (report twice a week) and then a lot of training.

I was excited, I grew up in Mt. Pleasant. My wife and I had most of our family in the Charleston area. I reported to Charleston Naval Base in early May following travel from Idaho to South Carolina with a little leave thrown in for good measure. When I reported for duty, I was sent to see the Blue and Gold Crew detailers, a couple of Chiefs (E-7). I knew something was up when the Blue Crew detailer told the Gold "I got an ELT." I was shuffled over to the barracks, given a job to keep me busy until the Key picked me up, and then sent home for the day.

I got called later that day and told to get ready to go to sea. The USS Lewis & Clark SSBN-644 Gold was short an ELT, was going to sea in a couple of days, and I was going to be on her. I had a couple of days to get everything in order, get my gear together, and report to the ship.

The day to report onboard arrived, and my wife took me to the Charleston Naval Weapons Station to pick up the boat. She escorted me as far down the dock as possible and I actually met the sailor I was replacing. He was removed from the boat for disciplinary reasons and would soon be discharged from the Navy. At least I had an idea why I was short cycled to the sea.

I checked in topside and was escorted below. I was hooked up with a PO 2, another new ELT. He was really salty; he had been with the boat about three months doing part of off-crew time and made sea trials. I was allowed to use a rack for the night since half the crew had that last night off before going to sea. Bright and early the next morning I started my first patrol able to locate the crews head, crews mess, and berthing. I do not remember where they stuck me for the maneuvering watch.

The first patrol was two months of two a day drills for Engineering in desperate preparation of an Operational Readiness Safety Examination (ORSE), intense study for engineering qualifications, and intense study for submarine qualifications. When we turned the boat over to the blue crew two months later, I was the last watch stander relieved. I literally had to run to catch the bus to the airport. My first patrol was a blur. We managed to fail the ORSE.

Naturally, I found out why I was sent to the Clark instead of the Key. For example, the Leading ELT MM1 (SS) had left his radiation badge on his rack and missed my first patrol. He was awarded E-5 and a tin can out of Charleston. There was also a MMC (SS) ELT that missed sea trials. He was masted and lost a bunch of money, since he was a Chief he remained a Chief. He made the patrol but was rotated off the boat as soon as we flew back to Charleston. I was also given the legend of eight ELT's before me that left one way or another to escape the Clark. She was NOT a happy boat for the nukes, particularly the ELTs.

The "Leakie and Creakie" was not all bad. The E-5 nuke mafia were a bunch of great guys and I made some great friends. I did the normal stuff like tie a string across the boat outside my duty station and watch it drop as the boat submerged. On the deep dives it was very impressive. When you are down, you can stretch the string taut and watch it snap on the way back up. The boat made a LOT of noise as it made depth transients. This occurred as the hull compressed or relaxed. Loud sudden noises still make me look up expecting to see a problem with the submarine hull.

Saturday nights were casino nights. The crews mess served pizza through the evening and some forms of gambling were allowed. The winnings, and the house always wins, went into the recreation fund. There are so many things that I can remember about the five patrols I made. We drank "bug juice" which was like Kool Aid, and we also had a soda machine on board. To get a check out back in the engine room I quickly learned that a pitcher of bug juice and a pitcher of soda really greased the skids.

On one patrol the CO_2 ran out for the soda machine, so the NUC engineered a way to get other compressed gases on the machine. The taste was very funky. As a bonus, I learned to mix orange bug juice with half the water and use the solution to clean deck plates in the engine room. The double strength bug juice really etched the steel deck plates; they came out nice and clean with no oxidation. When we loaded stores onboard the boat for patrol it was an all hands evolution. On my second patrol we diverted a lot of stuff back aft into engineering for the nukes. We had bags of cookies, cans of peanuts and cases of hot chocolate mix hidden all over the engine room. That was the last stores load that went down the hatch and they even stationed a Chief topside to guard the goodies.

I lived in a tube. The Lewis & Clark was 425 feet long and 33 feet in diameter at its largest point. Inside this tube, the Navy jammed weapons, habitation equipment, a nuclear propulsion plant, and sailors. The official party line was she was faster than 20 knots and dove deeper than 400 feet. We shared our berthing with the ships weapons systems. There were a couple of racks in a little box in the torpedo room, a couple of berthing cubicles in the missile compartment, and a berthing compartment for the rest of the crew. Since we really did not have enough racks for all the crew a couple of lucky non-rates, E-2 and E-3's, got to sleep in any flat space in the torpedo room and between missiles tube in lower level Missile Compartment.

The Clark carried 16 Poseidon missiles in what is known as "Sherwood Forest". You step through a hatch and see two, long rows of tubes. The crew was divided into three distinct groups, "Noseconers or Coners," "Weaponeers," and "Nukes." The Coners work in the front part of the boat and include Auxiliary Division (A-Gang). This group included Sonarmen, Radiomen, non-nuclear Electronic Technicians, Torpedomen, Mess Management Specialist (cooks), and A-Gang. The A-Gangers were non-nuclear machinist mates that operated and maintained non-nuclear machinery all over the boat. The Weaponeers included the Fire Control Technicians and Missile Technicians, they baby sat the nuclear missiles. Then there were the Nukes in the back of the boat known as Disney Land Aft. The Nukes were the kings of the nuclear propulsion plant. Each group had their own unique tribal lore and tendencies, but they were all submariners.

A submarine is a dangerous environment. This is a ship, boat, that was designed to sink; a good day is when you surface one time than you dove. The boat carried torpedoes, explosive packed mini submarines, with their own unique and very toxic fuel mix. The 16 Poseidon missiles had the ability to carry multiple warheads on each missile. If a missile rocket motor decided to ignite in the tube, the boat would melt down in a matter of seconds.

The boat also carried environmental control equipment. One machine was used to extract oxygen and hydrogen from sea water. We needed the oxygen, but the hydrogen was dumped overboard. We called the machines "bombs;" more than one let go in the fleet. In the engine room we had steam, produced using the reactor, to power all of the propulsion and electrical generating equipment. The reactor also produced and shared radiation with the entire crew but primarily with the nukes.

I belonged to two engineering divisions on the boat. I was a MM in Machinery (M) Division and an ELT in Reactor Laboratories (RL) Division. There were only 4 ELT's on board and up to 16 MM's total to stand watches. I had to qualify basic nuclear operator (all the nuclear theory stuff and many of the basic system) and qualify to stand watches on the various watch stations. I stood ELT watch which ran 24/7. When it was my turn, I would be duty ELT for weeks at a time.

There was a set routine of stuff you had to do each day, so it was up to the Duty ELT to work around the ships routine and get everything done. The other watch stations were stood for six hours at a time depending on the watch schedule. I qualified Auxiliary Machinery Room 2 Lower Level (AMR2LL), Engine Room Upper Level (ERUL) and Lower Level (ERLL) (also known as Lower Level Louie), and Engine Room Supervisor (ERS). The junior M-Division watch station was Lower Level Louie and for the ELT naturally Duty ELT. A good watch rotation was 6 and 12, 6 hours on watch and 12 hours off. I spent a lot of time in Port and Starboard, 6 on and 6 off in AMR2LL and ERLL. During your off watch time you worked on qualifications, did required maintenance, attended training, ate, and grabbed what sleep you could.

Submarine qualifications are rigorous qualifications. I was issued a qualification card with a list of systems and practical factors that I was required to perform. The process was to study everything you could about the system and be able to draw it. You also walked it down and put your hand on all the important parts that were accessible. Then you went to a subject matter expert (SME) and got a checkout. You were required to demonstrate to the SME you knew enough about the system. We were required to understand how the submarine operated, how to operate a lot of the equipment on board, and to fight any causality, fire, flooding, weapons accidents, etc., in each compartment. You stood topside security watch, drove the submarine underway, and demonstrated you could rig any compartment for any problem. I got to fire a torpedo tube; actually, I really only impulse water out the tube. But then I got to get into the tube and wipe it down.

Once you got all of your signatures, you did a walk-through of the submarine with the Chief of the Boat or the Executive Officer. During the walkthrough you answered any question they decided to ask or demonstrated how to operate any equipment they pointed out. Then you went to a qualification board of three crusty submarine sailors that again tested your knowledge.

When you finally satisfied everyone with your level of knowledge, you were awarded your Submarine Warfare Pin also known as dolphins or fish. Mine were pinned on by the Commanding Officer in the back of the crews mess. Once pinned you walked through the mess. The Chief's table was the first table on the mess deck. One young 'A' Ganger was pinned at the same time. As he walked past the Chief's table this meaty fist appeared and tacked on his fish. The Chief broke the fish in two, implanted the two parts in the kids chest, and put the kid on the deck. It was good to be a nuke at times.

Engineering qualifications was more of the same. We were required to demonstrate detailed knowledge of all the nuclear theory. We learned all about the various systems associated with the reactor plant; we learned to draw the system, know all the setpoints and important parameters, demonstrate location of components, and construction of components. We took a written test to demonstrate knowledge and stood watches under instruction to demonstrate we understood the watch station. This was followed by an in-depth oral examination by the Engineer and for some, an interview with the Captain.

The bottom line is the qualifications were rigorous and no one remained on the boat unless they were qualified. Every man on a submarine is important. There are many systems were one man making a mistake could bring disastrous consequences. A submariner feared two things, fire and flooding. There was nowhere to run. The nukes got an added bonus, steam. A nuclear submarine uses the reactor to make steam which in turn is used to operate the propulsion plant. If a major steam leak occurred in your compartment, you could get boiled alive if it were not stopped fast enough or you did not escaped the compartment.

Submarines were known for having the best food. I can say this is a yes and no thing. My first two patrols, the Mess Chief was an old fashion submarine sailor. He fed us good. We had "surf and turf" a couple of times during the runs and the food was always plentiful and well prepared. On my third patrol we had a changing of the Chiefs and a skimmer (surface Navy) Chief came on board to cross train as a submariner. He came off a tin can and this did not go well. He was determined to balance the food budget, so the quality and quantity suffered. We even ran out of food one a patrol. The food was lousy. This resulted in a food riot on board. The Executive Officer set up a food committee with members from each division to approve the menus and provide suggestions.

Many people ask me if I got claustrophobic. It never bothered me. It was just a strange way to make a living. We did have a couple of guys get really agitated and wanting to get some fresh air. When this happened you just talked them down. We had one guy on patrol "lose the bubble." He spent the rest of the patrol drugged up in the Torpedo Room under constant observation of the Torpedo Room watch stander. During the early days of nuclear submarines, the psychiatrists decided we could be kept sane underwater for long periods if we had an ice cream machine. So, the Leakie and Creakie had an ice cream machine; I'm not sure how much this really helped.

Life on a sub boiled down to three days: yesterday, today, and tomorrow. You knew the time of day from the food being served and the events. During my entire time aboard the sub, we drilled Monday through Friday during the 1200 to 1800 watch. If we had drills, it would have been the afternoon. Every Friday during the 0600 to 1200 we would have some type of ships drill that got everyone up. This is the only time that the lights in berthing were turned on. The end result was rub-a-dub-dub, clean up the sub. The nice thing was sliders were always served for lunch and the afternoon drills were minor engineering drills. The drills during Monday through Thursday were always major catastrophes.

One of the facts of life in the military are drills, at least in the Navy. We practiced or drilled on anything that could damage the sub or the reactor plant. Most drills were fully simulated like a fire. Others, such as a reactor scram (controls rods inserted and reactor shutdown) went from a drill to the real thing as soon as the reactor was shut down. We also drilled on ship wide casualties and manned battle stations for both torpedo attacks and missile launches.

This particular drill really stood out for me. When we manned battle stations missiles, the Captain always came on the 1MC and announced this is the Captain and this is an exercise. Well, the word came over the 1MC to man battle stations missile, but we had no word from the Captain this was an exercise. It really sank in that if this was the real thing, the Russians had launched nuclear weapons against the United States. We were stationed and lived in Charleston, SC. There were a number of prime targets in this city, the Charleston Air Force Base, the Charleston Naval Base, the Charleston Naval Shipyard, and the Naval Weapons Station. It was a very high probability that our home would be gone, turned into a radioactive wasteland. After about 30 minutes the Captain finally announced that it was a drill and we stood down. It taught me what our job was in the big picture. Nuclear warfare is for keeps.

After two and half years, I rotated off the boat. The boat was heading to the yards, and I did not want to go. I traded an advanced school and extended a couple of months for shore duty. I was transferred to the Nuclear Power Training Unit (NPTU) in Ballston Spa, New York. I spent three and a half years training both officer and enlisted students in the art and science of operating a Naval nuclear power plant. The prototype was tough. The students worked twelve hours a day on a rotating seven day schedule. We did seven days of mid-shift, seven days of swing shift and then seven days of days. The staff got more breaks, but we still worked a lot of twelve hour training days.

I was discharged from the Navy in May 1984 after serving 8 years, 2 months and 29 day, but who counted. I started class at Clemson using my GI Bill benefits while I was on separation leave. One thing I quickly found was I missed the people. Submariners and nukes are different people. I tried a one year enlistment in the Army National Guard as a student. It didn't really click, and I decided I would like to complete my 20 years in the Navy. I went through all the testing and screening to enter a Navy officer program but was only offered a reserve position (age related) which would have required a lot of training with no guaranteed follow on assignment.

In December 1987, I graduated from Clemson University as a Mechanical Engineer. Since a Naval career was not a guarantee I opted to go to work in the civilian sector. I did a very short tour at Newport News Shipyard as a design engineer on the Seawolf submarine project. This job just did not click, glorified copy boy, so I went to work at Charleston Naval Shipyard as a nuclear engineer. My code provided direct support to the nuclear fleet. As an engineer at the shipyard, I learned about the Naval Reserve Engineering Duty Officer (EDO) program. Based on my degree and my grades from Clemson, I was awarded a direct commission as an Ensign in the Naval Reserve.

As an EDO I was assigned to a Charleston Naval Shipyard reserve unit as a ship repair specialist. We trained to become Ship Superintendents for ship and submarine repair and overhaul. I attended an "intense" two day "knife and fork school" to learn how to be an officer and then the Naval Reserve Engineering Duty Officer School. We did our annual training at the shipyard. The Navy did not know what to do with us.

I did a couple of two week annual training periods doing strange projects but finally got assigned to submarine overhauls. Eventually the peace dividend caught up with me; the shipyard was shut down, and I ended up in a reserve weapons station unit at Charleston Naval Weapons Station. The weapon station units trained to handle all the conventual munitions for destroyers and cruisers and all the big stuff to keep a Marine happy. In addition to training for an active duty position as Weapons Safety Officer, I also served as the Training Officer in one weapons station unit and the Executive Officer in my second unit.

My civilian career took me from Charleston Naval Shipyard to a nuclear utility, and then the Department of Energy (DOE) at Savannah River Site (SRS). As mentioned, the peace dividend got me once and was about to get me again, and I was sure I was gone. One of my fellow engineers at SRS was a Lt. Colonel in the Army Reserve; he had the office next to mine. One afternoon, after I had just gotten off the phone with the Reserve Center in Charleston, he stuck his head in my office and told me he had billets in his unit and would pay me until I was ready to retire.

So, a couple of months later I took the bait and went from the Naval Reserve to the Army Reserve. I resigned my commission as a Lieutenant (O-3E) in the Naval Reserve and accepted a commission as a Captain (O-3E) in the Army Reserve. I was assigned to a special design unit in the 416th Engineers. The Army Reserve owns a bunch of sites, and they required engineering support. I did a lot of work for the Army Reserve; they kept me very busy. I also moved around in the government working with both the DOE and the Nuclear Regulatory Commission (NRC). My civilian jobs took me through various facets of nuclear power plant operation, nuclear weapons materials, and nuclear weapons.

In the Army Reserve, I competed the Army Engineering Officer Advanced Course and was later promoted to Major. Once I hit the twenty-one year point, I told the Colonel I was ready to retire. That was August 2001. Well, in September, I was taking a nuclear engineering course in boiling water reactors at the NRC training facility when two aircraft were flown into the World Trade Center. On a break in the TV room, we watched a 767 fly into one of the towers. I let the Colonel know I would stay on board until we found out if we would get mobilized or not. Within a year it was clear we would not get mobilized and my civilian job at nuclear power plants was getting very intense because of security upgrades. So, in 2002, I transferred to the Retired Reserve.

At age 60 in 2014, I formally retired from the US Army, actually Army of the United States, and started receiving my retired pay. In 2016, I retired from the DOE and moved to Anderson, SC. I am very active in my church where I currently lead the Men's Ministry, work in the middle school ministry, and perform projects both in and for the church. When this was written, I have been married to my high school sweetheart for 49 years and have two children, a boy and a girl. God has been so good to me!

Through my church I was introduced to Vets Helping Vets Anderson. VHVA gave me a sense of belonging as a veteran that I did not have before. The organization made me proud of my service to the nation and introduced me to a lot of great veterans. Through Vets Helping Vets, I was recruited into American Legion Post 184. This post has an Honor Guard that performs military honors at veterans funerals and flag ceremonies as requested. The Honor Guard keeps me very busy.

Robert Gilreath

I was born the only child of two hardworking textile workers in Anderson, South Carolina on March 18. 1947. My parents named me Robert Lee Gilreath. In 1965 when I went to work at the Anderson Fire Department, the guys started calling me Speck. The Porter Wagner Show was a popular weekly television program that featured country music stars and a comedian by the name of Speck Rhodes.

Both of my parents worked in the cotton mill at different shifts so that someone would always be at home to care for me. I learned at an early age how to prepare my own breakfast, get myself ready to walk the three-fourths mile to the Cleo Bailey Elementary school house. My chore was to remember to fill the coal or wood bucket so we could have heat in the house the next morning. I played outside until after the streetlight lit up the corner of the street. I am thankful I grew up on the mill village when the streets were safe, and kids were taught responsibility and respect. I eventually got a bicycle to ride to McCants Junior High, and started T.L. Hanna High School in 1962, the first year they put the boys and girls together.

When I turned sixteen I got my driver's license and worked at Dempsey's Shell Service Station. It was a full service filling station where I made fifty cents an hour. With the help of my dad, I bought a 1955 Ford with the four hundred dollars I saved from working while attending school. I took textiles in school but when I graduated, Dad talked to some people he knew about getting me on at the fire department. I had to go around and talk to some council members, the mayor, and the Fire Chief. That was the process back in those days to get a job with the city.

I met my wife, Vicki, in 1965. I had a motorcycle and she enjoyed riding with me. I told her I was being drafted and if she were not married when I came back, I would look her up. When I came back in 1968, we started dating and married in 1970. We have one daughter and a grandson.

My grandfather served in WWI and my dad served in WWII. So, with Vietnam heating up, I was preparing to be drafted. My Dad's brother, Prue Gilreath was wounded in WWII. He taught me a lot about life and war. I was drafted into the United States Army on July 6, 1966. In basic training, we got up early. Something I was already use to. We had to eat and drink what they gave you. I remember there was a soda fountain with Coca Cola or Pepsi set up. As trainees we were told it was off limits. Sure, was tempting for some, but we followed the rules to keep out of trouble and to respect their authority. Something the youth of today might have a hard time with. The lesson behind our instructor's orders where simple. If we obeyed orders in the small things there was a good chance when it came to the larger things we could be trusted to follow them, also.

From Basic Training at Fort Jackson, South Carolina, I went to Fort Rucker, Alabama for Advance Individual Training. I trained at the Army Aviation school as a fixed-wing mechanic and then rotary wing mechanic on the Huey helicopters. I received a nine-day leave and then sent to Fort Ord, California for shots. Next destination was Vietnam by airplane. We arrived January 1, 1967, and were taken straight to board a bus with a wire cage around it.

Our first glimpse of what lay ahead were the six wounded soldiers they were unloading from a Huey. Some on stretchers with injuries hard to erase from my head. I prayed every day for safety, and I thanked the Lord for bringing me home. I was not physically wounded while serving in Vietnam, but my wounds go deep. They wake me up with night terrors. I am easily startled by loud noises or being jostled awake.

My assignment in Vietnam was to do ninety percent of the maintenance on the aircraft. When it left the ground, I was sitting in the side manning a machine gun. I laugh now and say they knew we were in good shape, if I was willing to jump on and fly with them as their door gunner. We did not have a particular station. Our job was a solid year of fighting for our nation. We slept out in the field or in a shop long enough to get flying to our next destination. We would fly from the coast of South Vietnam to the side left of Cambodia by nightfall. Seasons and weather patterns were different for each place. It was usually wet and hot, but we could fly over to a spot where the temperature was 40-50 degrees and pouring rain, It felt like it was 30 degrees to us. Our bodies had gotten use to the hot humid weather, sometimes 110 degrees in the sunshine.

It was around Christmas when I was preparing to go home from my year of service in Vietnam. Nancy Sinatra landed at the airfield for the Bob Hope Christmas Show. She was famous for her song, "These Boots Are Made For

Walking." This song meant something else for American soldiers in Vietnam marching in combat boots.

I spent the rest of my time in the military working on the flight line at the Hunter Army Airfield at the base in Savannah, Georgia. I had only one Sergeant over me. Around one hundred choppers needed to be checked and ready to fly the next morning. Old pilots trained new pilots with practical jokes such as telling them to check the play in the rotors or the water in the radiator.

Even before I was drafted, I knew the military was a good place to learn self-discipline like making your own bed and caring for your own clothes. My advice to our youth today is: Stop whining and grow up, show some responsibility and respect without being made to, and realize men and women sacrificed their lives for the freedoms you enjoy.

The Anderson City Fire Department allowed me to come back to work when I returned home after my time in the Army in 1968. I started out as a tail board man riding on the back of the firetruck. Worked my way up to engineer, the driver and then the Battalion Chief. I retired from the department after forty-four years of service as a fireman.

I also worked with veteran Gary Acker on my days off from the fire department. He was a valued Vets Helping Vets Anderson member and good friend. We lost Gary, March 1, 2021. Our families spent a lot of fun times together on vacations. Our faith in the Lord is what we knew allowed us to get through the things we endured. Gary and I found out about Vets Helping Vets Anderson through a mutual friend, veteran Tommy Lowe.

Then Sarge Sanchez a Korean War veteran, told me VHVA was a good organization. I joined and participated with the lawn care and ramp building team. Now Tommy Lowe, Mike Hawkins and I have the pleasure of taking other veterans out fishing. We try to take about six veterans out on the VHVA pontoon each Thursday, when weather permits. This gives us all a chance to discuss things with like-minded veterans in a smaller group and if we catch fish that is a plus. Some confess fishing is something they have missed while others admit they have never been fishing before.

Barry Gray

My name is Barry Lee Gray, and I was living in Duanesburg, a small town in Schenectady County, New York. I was drafted, and on April 24, 1969, I began my service in the United States Army. I found basic training to be OK, if you were in shape and could learn to follow orders.

My memory does not recall any funny moments of boot camp. I served in Vietnam in the 101st Airborne Division, 2/501st Infantry, Northern I Corp as a radio operator. I was awarded the rank of Sergeant (SGT.E5) and saw combat often. Over time most of the battalion was killed or wounded.

When we were leaving Vietnam, we received our debriefing. Then we were taken to another location to receive our medals and/or citations. We were issued a piece of paper with our name rank and unit. This stated what medals or citations we were to receive. There were no ceremonies, just pick up your medals and citations off the table.

Assigned to the Army Signal Corps, I was in charge of the distribution of codes for the radio operators in the battalion. I had to be precise in my objectives. This was not a full-time position, so, I also served as a radio operator in the field. Later I served in the forward tactical operations at the forward fire bases. The main thing I found out about being a radio operator in the field or forward fire base was that you always had to be accurate on your radio transmissions when calling for support, et cetera. I had to be able to make fast, precise decisions, in split seconds, especially in combat situations.

I honorably processed out of the military from Fort Bragg, North Carolina. My last assignment was with company B 25th SIG Battalion. I was discharged in April of 1971 in a quick and normal way.

It was great to get home. I was proud that I served and was able to return. Military service left me jumpy, and I was always watching the movement of people that were near or around me. It took me some time to get used to being with groups of people in close quarters. I hesitated answering questions from people or friends that never served or had seen combat. I was always afraid if I told them what it was really like, they would not believe me and think that I was making it up. So, I rarely mentioned anything about combat. I did tell them to join the military and they would find out about it themselves. I had no problem speaking to a former veteran who had seen combat.

I wanted my children to know about my military service and understand the citations and medals that I was awarded. I had four framed displays made-up from Medals of America, Simpsonville, South Carolina. I printed a list of explanations for the awards I was presented for my time in the US Army. This way they will know about it and be able to pass it on to their children in the future. This is a list along with the explanations:

Army Presidential Unit Citation - This citation is awarded to units who demonstrate exceptional heroism in the action against an armed enemy. Requirements include that the unit must "display such gallantry, determination, and spirit in accomplishing its mission

106

under extremely difficult and hazardous conditions as to set it apart from and above other units in the same campaign."

Army Meritorious Unit Citation - This citation is awarded to units of the United States Army who show exceptional meritorious conduct in their performance of duties for a period of at least six months during conflict with an armed enemy. While service in a combat zone, their service must be directly related to the combat effort.

Republic of Vietnam Civil Action Unit Citation - This citation was a declaration presented by the government of South Vietnam to recognize a units outstanding civic service to the state or civil service of great asset to the South Vietnamese cause. U.S. military units who were eligible for this citation generally participated in local police activity to contain civil unrest in areas of South Vietnam.

Bronze Star Medal - This medal is an award presented to service members who show acts of heroism in the field, or who are meritorious in their work. To qualify, service members must perform these acts during an armed conflict against an enemy of the United States. This award is the fourth highest combat award in the armed forces.

Army Commendation Medal - this medal is awarded to any member of the Armed Forces of the United States, other than General Officers who, while serving in any capacity with United States Army after

December 6, 1941, distinguished themselves by heroism, meritorious achievement or meritorious service.

Good Conduct Medal - This medal is given to any enlisted United States Army personnel who carry out consecutive years of "honorable and faithful service." Such service insinuates that a standard enlistment was achieved without any non-judicial punishments, disciplinary infractions, or court martial offences.

National Defense Service Medal - This medal is awarded to every member of the United States Armed Forces who has served during any one of four specified periods of armed conflict or national emergency from 1950 to present.

Vietnam Service Medal - This medal was awarded to all members of the United States Armed Forces who served in the Vietnam War Campaign, after July 4, 1965.

Vietnam Campaign Medal - this medal is awarded to recognize service during the Vietnam War by all members of the United States Armed Forces.

Expert Marksman Rifle Badge - Qualifying as an "expert marksman" is no extraordinary achievement for soldiers in the army. In basic training and usually once a year, soldiers have to qualify for their service weapon period to earn their expert badge, they must hit 36 out of 40 targets from distances of 50 to 300 meters.

Phil Harris

My name is Philip Joel Harris. I was born in Clinton, South Carolina on January 14, 1948. My family moved to Anderson, South Carolina when I was about five years old. I grew up in Anderson and attended McDuffie High School and graduated from high school in early June 1967. I joined the Army on June 12, 1967, and endured Basic Training at Fort Gordon, Georgia. After basic, I took my Advanced Individual Training (AIT) at Fort Sill, Oklahoma as a Fire Direction Control Technician for Heavy Artillery. In other words, I laid out the direction that the big guns were to shoot. Fortunately for the infantry, I was not assigned to that duty in Vietnam.

After AIT, I was sent to Vietnam and assigned to the 5th Automatic Weapons Battalion, 2nd Artillery. This unit consisted of three Batteries of M42 Dusters (A Self-Propelled Anti-Aircraft Gun), Quad-50 Gun Trucks and an artillery searchlight battery. These three Duster batteries were assigned to three Infantry Divisions, the 9th Infantry Division which covered the Mekong River Delta, the 25th Infantry Division which covered the area West of the Iron Triangle, and the 1st Infantry Division (The Big Red One) which covered the area east of the Iron Triangle. My Battery was assigned to the Big Red One. The 1st Division is the oldest and one of the most recognized units of the Army and the only Division that has been continuously active since the First World War.

A Duster was a light armored vehicle with an open turret that housed twin 40mm cannons. As I had no training on this weapon, I had to settle for on-the-job training. This meant that the first firefight that I was involved in was the first time that I fired the guns on my track, considering I did not know how to load them.

Our duties consisted of escorting convoys and clearing Highway 13 in the morning. Highway 13 was nicknamed Thunder Road. Our duties also consisted of perimeter security on different fire bases up and down Highway 13. Highway 13 in Vietnam run through the middle of the Michelin Rubber Plantation.

I was wounded on September the 13th of 1968. We were ambushed on Highway 13 while sweeping the road that morning with a platoon of infantry. My track was apparently the target for RPG (rocket propelled grenade). Luckily, the RPG hit a bush beside the road and exploded instead of hitting the track. My Track Commander and I were hit by the shrapnel. I do not remember a whole lot initially after that except for the fact that I was scared. Then it really pissed me off. We returned fire with the infantry and Track Commander. A couple of the infantry and I were dusted off, but fortunately none of us were killed.

When my tour was over on November 6, 1968, I came home for thirty days leave. And subsequently assigned to a basic training company at Fort Bliss, Texas. The Major General presented me with a Purple Heart which became more important to me through the years. The reason I was assigned to a basic training company was because the Army and their intelligent manner thought I needed to be a Drill Sergeant. I did not have a choice. If I flunked out, they would bust me, so I did the best I could and graduated third out of a class of forty. I got promoted to a buck sergeant (E-5) at that time. Sergeant First Class Carrera was my senior instructor at drill sergeant school. He was a physically big man and sharp as a tac. We would joke about him having chrome plated field gear. He encouraged me to do my best and respected what I did in Vietnam. After a year and a half, Fort Bliss transferred me to Fort Dix, New Jersey. I stayed there until I got out of the Army in 1970.

When I got home, I had a hard time trying to fit in, because everybody was acting like nothing had ever happened. Like they were unaware of the death and destruction we had seen and been through. I first started drinking a lot and I had several jobs. I could not fit in because no one seemed to know what even happened in Vietnam.
I basically became an alcoholic and had trouble keeping jobs when I was not able to get up in the morning.

I straightened up a little and went back to school and earned an associate degree in engineering graphics at Tri-County Technical College, while I was working at Saco-Lowell, a manufacturing plant in Easley, South Carolina. I enrolled for a semester in Clemson. Even after attending school, I still had no purpose and just bummed around without committing to one job. I spent fifteen years of my life, in an absolutely foolish way, until I met my wife, Rachel. Rachel and the grace of God saved my life. Having a good mate encouraged me. I stopped drinking about forty years ago. My beverage of choice now is sweet tea and Mountain Dew. Rachel and I have children and grandchildren who we are very proud of. I retired from the U.S. Post Office when I was sixty-two.

The thing that really bothers me is that I cannot remember the guys that were in Vietnam with me. It is like it has been rubbed out or erased from my mind. The VA doctor explained that this can be a normal reaction for somebody that has seen death. It is survival for some by getting it out of their mind.

I am still alive, thank the Lord, although I just do not feel I am any better with my Post-Traumatic Stress Disorder (PTSD). I find it is hard to get better after all I and others like me went through. Meeting with the Combat Veterans on Monday nights, and Vets Helping Vets on Wednesdays gives me a chance to express myself and listen to others who share the same trials. Hopefully, we can be there for each other and the younger soldiers who have seen combat.

I have met others whom I admire such as Jesse Taylor whose vision and perseverance kept us together. We met at the VA as part of the original fourteen. Bob Robinson, a VHVA member is the most hardworking man I have ever met. He was a combat medic and has a big heart for those in need.

I played the drums and sang in a band with Ronnie Roper, a talented musician and fellow Vietnam Vet when we both got back home to Anderson. I got back from Vietnam before Ronnie was sent over. We sent occasional letters to spur each other on. He is a longtime friend and fellow VHVA member.

Vets Helping Vets Anderson has given me a purpose. Working with others on the Lawn Crew, I have a sense of accomplishment. I know we are helping other veterans who deserve our help. I thank the good Lord for all the blessings He has given me.

Mike Hawkins

My name is Michael Lloyd Hawkins. The teens in my church call me Hawk. I was living on R Street in the Appleton Mill Village of Anderson, South Carolina when I was drafted on April 16, 1969.

Basic training was not a big problem for me because I was athletic. I realized early that if I did just what I was told, everything would go well. My drill instructor, SSgt. Emerson Boozer was a heavyweight boxing champ on our base at Fort Jackson, South Carolina. He gave me no trouble because I always responded to him correctly. He did beat a guy very bad in front of everyone to make an example of him. The guy became a good soldier after that. When I graduated from basic, I was awarded a stripe. Only three of us got one.

I recall a funny moment. On graduation day my first sergeant called me to his office and said, "Hawkins, I just noticed that you have not pulled any duty the whole time you have been here. Who did you pay to keep you off the duty roster? I replied, "No one, Sir! I just do what I am told." He replied, "OK, then you will be in the mess hall all day today." I said, "Sir, my wife and parents are coming to see me graduate today." He said, "Your people will not recognize your bald head on that field." So, I worked in the mess hall all day.

Here is the funny part, although it was not funny at the time. I was dining room orderly (DRO) for all the officers and NCO's coming to eat. I would take their order, get their food, and serve them at their table. Well, our Commanding Officer

(CO), Captain Kline came in and gave me his order. I got him a tray of food and went to his table to deliver it. As I was setting the tray down, a small bowl of lima beans slid across the tray and dumped into his lap!

He erupted into a rage because he had his dress uniform on, and of course, he is the CO. He cursed and I thought he might hit me, but he finally stormed off. I was starting to pick up the mess when someone tapped me on my back. I turned around to see my first sergeant who asked, "Hawkins, why did you throw those beans in the captain's lap? To which I replied, "Sir, I did not throw them on him. It was an accident." He then said, "I think you did it because I had you pull duty today. Do I need to take you outside and stomp you?" I replied, "Sir, whatever you choose to do, I'm OK with it."

He just turned and left me to clean up the mess. The next day as we were leaving, he called me out of formation and handed me a stripe. With a grin he said, "If you had broken on me yesterday, I would not have given you this."

Adapting to military life was not hard for me because I was already taught at home to show respect for my elders. My advanced training was at Fort Eustis, Virginia where I was taught maintenance on Light Observation Choppers (OH6As) also known as Skeeters or Little Birds.

Vietnam was my next stop in September of 1969. I remember flying into Saigon and seeing all the bomb craters across the landscape then wondering how I could live here for a year and not be one. I was assigned to 123rd War Lords on a flight line in Chulai, Vietnam.

The front door of my hooch opened to the flight line and the back door opened to a beautiful beach and reef. My job was crew chief on a Skeeter. I only did this for a couple of weeks because I was more afraid of GI's on drugs than the enemy. Help was needed in the hangar to keep the maintenance up on the choppers, so I volunteered to be a mechanic. They were happy to get me and gave me another stripe. Soon the squad leader DEROZED (a term used when you depart or leave an assignment) and went home. No one wanted his position, so I took it. They gave me another stripe. They were so pleased at how we kept the Little Birds flying, I soon was awarded another stripe. I was now Specialist 4 working in an E-6 position.

What I remember most about this time was leaving the Anderson County Airport on a DC3 and saying goodbye to my lovely young wife Kay. May 1st through the 3rd, we got hit at daylight with 122mm rockets. We jumped up and ran to get in our sandbag shelters. Praise the Lord, no one got hit or hurt. On the second morning we were up and waiting. Sure enough, we got hit again. There was a problem when one of our guys who slept right beside me came out of the hooch last. He was high on drugs. We were the guards at the blast wall for our bunker. He came over to me and said tell everyone to get out of this bunker. This is mine. I called his name and said, "Herrigas! Man, they need to stay inside until the rockets stop." He shoved his M16 into my stomach and said, "Tell them to get out, or I will kill you." I turned and told those inside to get out and that this bunker was his. They filed out quickly.

One of them found First Sergeant and told him what was happening. First Sarge walked up behind Herrigas and used his own rifle as a bat to knock him out and down. He then had him chained in the office to a post. Sarge called me to his office at noon and asked me to get a couple of guys, take him, and beat him really bad to help him straighten up. I told Sarge if we do this, he will kill us one at a time. I continued, "If you cannot get rid of him, I will go to Thailand on my next flight, and go AWOL to the USA." Sarge had the MP's pick him up the next day and he was sent to jail.

As far as active combat, I never fired a shot at anyone. I did stop two men from entering our perimeter: one Vietnamese and one American GI. We had one helicopter go down because of a mechanical problem and all eleven men were burned to death. I had warned people about the crew chief who got a Dear John letter and was staying drunk and high. Not taking care of the Helo.

We also had one fellow soldier found dead right outside my hooch. He had been choked; I think by another soldier. Seeing all these soldiers on drugs, putting themselves and others in danger was the best deterrent for me not to ever try drugs.

A prank that I remember would be my first flight in a chopper turned out to be an auto rotation practice just to see if it scared me. Special activities for my friends and I were to trade the Navy guys our beer and cigarette rations for masks, snorkels, flippers, and spear guns. We would snorkel and shoot fish around the reefs. The first lobster I ever saw in my life, I shot and gave to a Vietnamese friend. We saw some beautiful sights on the reefs.

When I had been in country for a few months, I received word my brother was coming with a 3rd Marine Division. I tried to block him from coming but I could not. However, after he was in country for a few weeks, I was able to meet his CO on one of my flights into Da Nang. I asked him to allow my brother, Henry P. Hawkins, Jr., to come with me for a week on my base.

I do not know about any good luck, but God blessed me beyond my expectations by keeping me safe and sane. He allowed me to return home to a wonderful wife who I had the privilege of living with for 54 years.

Coming home was like a dream/nightmare. One day we are on high alert, watching everyone and everything around us and expecting trouble. The next day we are told to throw away our military clothes and get civilian clothes on as we travel home because of the troublemakers in and around airports we traveled through. Once home it took a few weeks to get accustomed to the change of atmosphere.

When I came home from Nam in September of 1970, I had a 30-day leave, then reported to Hunter Army Airfield in Savannah, Georgia, to finish out six months. I was asked over and over to re-up and offered bonuses to do so. I just wanted to be my own boss and plan my own schedules. Life at Hunter Air Force Base could be summed up as this: sleep, report to the hangar, play volleyball, drink coffee, and eat donuts.

I drove home almost every Friday after formation. Things were very loose, so one Friday I told my squad leader that I was going to stay home until someone missed me. The following Friday my squad leader called and said you were missed at formation this morning. I waited and came back to formation on Monday morning. First Sergeant asked me to stay after formation where he drilled me about being absent on Friday morning. My answer was that I just left a little early. I got an article 15, fined $50, and extended to serve for three extra days. They never realized I was gone for ten days! No one invaded the base while I was at home that week. A few weeks later, I received my separation papers, and I went home to stay.

My first few weeks back home were fun, and it was great getting back to all the things that were familiar. I enjoyed getting to know my wife better. I do not remember any real struggles other than sleeping very lightly, which I still do. I was often swinging a fist at anyone who startled me and woke me up.

After I was out of service for about a year, I fell in love with Jesus and began serving faithfully at a local church. After serving six years in this church, God drafted me to be a missionary for a 35-year period. I have now been on staff at my home church for six years.

My voice to those transitioning out of the military is if you are a Christian, find a good Bible preaching church and get involved with it. Military people make great servants of Jesus Christ. If you're not saved, please learn about the gospel and trust Jesus as your only way to heaven. **Eternity is too long to be wrong**.

My time in the military gave me confidence to be a leader and not a follower. I learned that I could do more than what is expected of me. My hope is to help many people, young and old, come to a decision of trust in Jesus Christ as their only way to get to heaven and spend eternity with God.

The only habit I picked up was drinking hard liquor which I dropped when Jesus took over my life. I can truly say I only miss getting to fly on choppers. It is hard to tell of all the temptations and distractions that you have to deal with as a young man.

I want my children and grands to know that I was drafted into the military. I was determined to do my duty for my country. to survive, and to return home. I did not run away, nor did I try to avoid it like Bill Clinton, former President of the United States, and others. I do believe Vietnam was a big mistake made by our politicians! What a big waste of many young lives, tons of equipment, and dollars. There was too much policing and not enough warring. Anytime America commits to go to war, it should be full force and do not hold back.

Darrell Massey kept inviting me to the Vets Helping Vets meetings. I kept saying I may come one day but I really did not intend to go. One day when he asked, I said I would be there tomorrow. It was not what I expected. I attended Am Vets when I first came home from the military. It was only a lot of drinking and partying, etc.

Vets Helping Vets Anderson is not a Sunday school or a substitute for church, but it is a great fellowship of friends with like-minded ideas. Everyone is not a Christian, but many are. Those who are struggling find help in our groups. I enjoy taking guys and gals fishing where they can relax, unwind, and talk through what is troubling them. My advice to them almost always comes from the word of God. Thank you for allowing me to share!

John 1:12 KJV: But as many as received him, to them gave he power to become the sons of God, even to them that believe on his name.

Sam Heaton

My name is Samuel L. Heaton. My nickname was Hoggbody because I was a fighter, with a bad attitude when cornered, and could survive in the mud and water. In 1968, I enlisted in the United States Army. I was living in Gadsden, Alabama with my wife Lysa, and our baby.

I enlisted in the military because I wanted to serve my country. I wanted to be the best fighter I could be. Basic training was rough because I had never been away from home. But the one thing that helped me make it through was that I had made a commitment to the greatest country in the world.

In Vietnam, I served the 9th Division in South Vietnam, assigned to Ranger Company E. Our areas of operations were the rivers and canals of the Mekong Delta. In Ranger Company G our areas of operation were in the Central Highlands. As a Special Force Ranger, we were part of the Hunter Killer Ambush in the Delta Long Range Reconnaissance Patrol in Central Highlands (LRRP).

I was awarded a Bronze Star with the Oak Leaf Cluster, Army Commendation with the Oak Leaf, Combat Infantryman Badge, Air Medal with Oak Leaf, and Purple Heart.

I recall Johnny Bench, a good friend and the best team leader. He was on his third deployment and had a house in Thailand. He had a nose for the enemy and could lead men. Friends and I enjoyed a drink and played volleyball during our downtime. I always recited Psalms 23: "…Yea, though I walk through valley of the shadow of death, I will fear no evil…when I faced difficulties and/or danger.

Coming home from combat, I was angry. I was screamed at and cussed at by the public. I became very angry knowing I could kill everyone that was cussing at me because I was very good at my job.

I left active duty in 1971 but continued with private contractors in US control. I had re-enlisted but was denied because of my combat involvement. I worked as a contractor for 10 years. When trying to find a job my private employer would not accept me back.

Due to my deployments with the military, I have several mental and physical problems. I am a patient with the VA. Many civilians do not understand the shaping of a person to be an effective and loyal soldier. It is hard to communicate emotions like dedication, anger, and revenge.

In the military, I learned organizational skills and the importance of the chain-of-command. I dislike war but want my family to know I served my country the United States of America with honor and believe in the United States Army motto: "This we'll defend." My hope is that the youth of today will develop a plan for their life. Be grateful for the blessings of freedoms they have due to the sacrifices of many who served in the military. Understand the importance of serving God, country, and family.

I enjoy hunting, catching crappies and bluegills.
Not many people have experienced the blessings and hardships I have scored on the inside and outside since I got

out of the Special Forces…but I love the Lord and our country.

Note: Vets Helping Vets member Tommy Lowe met veteran Sam Heaton, "Legends of the Outdoors" National Hall of Fame inductee, at the Grizzly Jig Show in Caruthersville, Missouri and asked him if he would participate in the VHVA veteran's story project. He replied, "Yes, if it will help the veterans."

Harry Humphrey

My name is Harry James Humphrey, Sr. I am the oldest of three children born to the late Harold and Lula Macy Humphrey. I was born and raised in Anderson, South Carolina, and I have been here all my life. I am a graduate of the old Westside High School class of 1965. My wife of 54 years, Betty Jean Johnson Humphrey, died in 2020. I do not have a nickname, but I am called Daddy, Granddaddy and Papa by my family. My great-granddaughter Taylor coined me Big Poppy

I enlisted in the Marine Corps in January 1967. Terry Nance, my childhood friend who was more like a Big Brother lived on the street behind me. I was always close to him and wanted to do all the things he did. I looked up to him and I guess you can say he was a role model for me. He was drafted for the military. He went to Vietnam and was wounded. I thought it was my duty to go over there and get the guys that hurt my Big Brother.

My boot camp was at Parris Island, South Carolina, and it was rough. We arrived at two or three o'clock in the morning. It was dark. The drill instructors jumped on the bus and started screaming and hollering to run everybody off the bus. When we got off the bus half the people were on one side of the bus and the other half of the people were on the other side of the bus. It was an eye opener and a shock.

I guess our funniest moments from boot camp was being named. You go through the training and do what you do. Then you got the stuff that we did which is funny now but was not too funny then. For example, the drill instructor would tell you to find his sand flea. So, you would find a sand flea. You brought it back to the drill instructor and he looks at you and says that was a female. You killed a male, find it. Then you find another one and bring it back for the DI to say that is a black one, and you killed the white one. Looking back, you know you went through that, and it becomes funny the things they did. They did not call us by our name. Their nick names for us was Maggots.

The military has changed as times changed. Drill Instructors cannot do all that stuff now. The military has become more political and kinder.

Adapting to military life involved getting up early in the morning and running everywhere we went. I didn't have a problem saying yes sir and no sir because that is the way I was raised to do it anyway. When you said sir, they would get on you and tell you that they work for a living. I would tell them I am not saying sir to your rank, I am saying sir to your age. I had to adapt to that because everything was sir to them. We were to say, "Sir, Private Humphrey request permission to do whatever." That was the way things went at Parris Island at boot camp.

The first war I served in was Vietnam. My job assignment was Infantry Rifleman. When I got to Vietnam in November 1967, I was assigned to the 2nd Battalion, 3rd Marine and 1st Marine Divisions. We were on what they call a float phase, which means we helped anybody that was in trouble. Someone gets on the horn and tells us that they need us. Our group gets on the helicopters and go in. We try to get everything calmed down. Then we get on another helicopter and go somewhere else to do the same thing. When I first got there, I walked point for two or three days. Then I walked tail-end Charlie for a while. As people got wounded, I advanced up to radio.

I was wounded in Vietnam on December 12, 1967. We were the lead squad that day and had three people in our squad. There was a point man, my squad leader who was walking second, and I was walking third with the radio. The place was called Guang Ngai in Vietnam. As we went over the hill and started down into the valley, I looked to my left side and saw a line of trees. Based on all the training that I had at Parris Island, South Carolina; Camp Lejeune, North Carolina; and Camp Pendleton, Florida; this was a clear sign of a possible attack.

I was not saved at that time. Mom and Daddy took me to church all my life. I had not dedicated my life to the Lord at that time, but I do know I heard the Lord say, "Ambush." I alerted my squad leader and said this would be a good place for an ambush.

Whether my point man tripped the booby trap, or the enemy threw a grenade, I do not know; but there was an explosion. The first round came in and hit me in the chest. My flak jacket stopped that one. I turned towards the tree line, picked up my radio, and started calling for help. I called, "Echo 1…Echo 1, this is Echo 2. Be advised that I made contact with the enemy, and I need some help!" They came back and said, "Echo 2…Echo 2, this is Echo 1. Be advised that we can't get to you right now."

127

Turning towards the tree line, I fired my first round out of my M16, and it jammed. I ejected it and fired a second round out of my M16, and it jammed again. Ejected again to fire a third round. When it jammed the third time, a bullet came and went through my right arm, ricocheted off of my flak jacket. One came in my right arm and then another grazed my face. It ricocheted off my flak jacket and opened my face up twice. Another one came in and got up under the radio. It bruised me but did not penetrate. I laid down with the right side of my face up and blood just flowed down my face.

All of a sudden, I felt my M16 come from under my body because I was laying on top of it. Normally when the Vietnam enemy comes up to you, the next thing they do is shoot you or cut your throat to ensure that you are dead. They left me and left us. I got hit four times. My squad leader got hit four times, but my point man got killed. We were just left out there. We were out there maybe 45 minutes to an hour before the helicopters came and medevacked us to the hospital in Da Nang.

I thought about when the enemy got the radio, the M16, grenades, and ammo. They got my ring and watch, then left me for dead. For a long time, I passed it off as luck but later on I knew that it was God that was protecting me. I looked back at the scripture, and it said Shadrach, Meshach, and Abednego were in the fiery furnace, but there was a fourth man in the furnace with them. There was a fourth man in that ambush with me that day and that fourth man was Jesus Christ. Even though I did not know him myself, that man was Jesus. I am alive today because Jesus Christ was in the fire with me that day. I will forever be grateful for his grace and mercy. I would like to encourage people that no matter the situation in life, the fourth man Jesus Christ is always with you going through the fire.

I spent thirty days in the hospital in Da Nang, then medevacked out to the hospital in Guam. I got wounded on December 12, 1967, and got to go to Guam in time to see Bob Hope's Christmas show. My cousin George Harrell was there at the Air Force Base in Guam, although I did not know this until several years after I got back. He said he was sitting right behind us, but we did not know it then. I was just trying to heal.

After leaving the hospital in Guam, I was sent to the Charleston Naval Hospital where I spent six months. After I recovered, I went back to Camp Lejeune, North Carolina. My wife went with me for a little while until we deployed on the cruise. She came back home while I actually finished up the training cruise. I got promoted to E5. About three months later, I was able to get out eleven months early.

We went to different places, including Panama, Virgin Islands, and St. Thomas to train and would be there for three months. The training cruise was on the USS Boxer. We repaired bunkers in Cuba. While on the cruise we would go out sometimes. The guys would go out on liberty (authorized absence), but I liked to pull shore patrol. If I pulled shore patrol, I would be able to go into the bar and get free drinks. I pulled shore patrol most of the time.

After I got out of the Marine Corps in 1970, I stayed out for three years. While I was in a class at Tri-County

Technical College in Pendleton, South Carolina, a young classmate told me that he was drilling that weekend with the National Guard. I told him I did not want anything to do with the military. He persuaded me to see how I would like it. I went to the drill that weekend. They talked me into it, and I joined the South Carolina National Guard with the 2-263rd Air Defense Artillery in the headquarters section.

I served many years as a E5. Then after a while I got promoted to E6 and I was transferred over to the guns. I didn't know anything about the M42 Duster. My crew people actually had to train me in what to do. We went from M42 Duster to the Stinger missiles. My Delta battery disbanded, and I went back to Headquarters battery.

I did not know anything about Headquarters because I was used to being in the field as a Sergeant doing things. I am a worker. We went to Camp Blanding, Florida; Fort Drum, New York; and Fort Bliss, El Paso Texas for training.

I guess the weirdest thing about the training was the Army sent evaluators to evaluate how good we were doing and if we knew our job. Most of these Army evaluators had never been anywhere and had no combat experience. They came out to watch us and tell us what we were doing right or wrong.

I remember one evaluator asked me, "Where's your alternate fighting position?" I just went on to gun because I didn't know what he was talking about. He asked, "Where are you going to if you get overrun at this position?" I looked at him and said, "I'm a Marine. We don't back up for anybody. We'll stay here and fight until the death." He didn't like my answer too much, so he asked me what I would do if I encountered an ambush. I asked him, "Do you want me to tell you what I'm gonna do or do you want me to tell you what the book says to do? What I'm going to do is get on the ground as low as I can and cover my butt!" I told him not to talk to me about what are you going to do because I was in an ambush in Vietnam. Sarge, I got the wounds and scars to prove it. I shed blood to prove what I am going to do in an ambush. I got on the ground as low as I could and covered myself the best I could in that ambush.

The Delta firing battery disbanded. About two years later, the Headquarters Battalion went to summer camp at Fort Jackson, South Carolina McCrady Training Center which is commonly called the Wet Site. We went to the field and First Sergeant came to me to tell me the Officer Candidate School (OCS) program was looking for some Technical Noncommissioned Officers (TAC NCOs), and Enlisted TAC NCOs. They preferred an E7 but would consider a sharp E6.

I was the sharp E6. We talked that day and the Colonel asked if I was gonna be free for the summer camp in two weeks. I told him I planned to be there because I was working at the post office, and it was no problem getting off work for the military. I went those two weeks of summer camp and enjoyed it because I got to harass want-to-be Lieutenants and have them crawl through the dirt and certain things like that. I really like being a TAC NCO. The next year I received a letter inviting me back as a TAC NCO for Phase One. I went back and did that for two weeks again.

The National Guard brought the Delta battery of the 263rd back. It was located in Pickens, SC because the National Guard had built four or five new armories to house the Hawk Missile Battalions. Colonel Nick Fletcher told me that I was being transferred to help bring the D Battery back online. I was the only person that would be transferring with a promotion because I was overlooked for too long. I was promoted to E7.

Out of the whole 2-263rd, we had four fire batteries, with four platoons in each, the headquarters battalion and the headquarters unit. I was the only black E7 in the 2-263rd at that particular time.

We had a company team school down at the Wet Site 218th Leadership. OCS was drilling the same weekend. I walked into the TAC Shack and Captain Hessey met me at the door. He told me there was an opening for a TAC NCO. The person they had in the position did not want it anymore.

Colonel let me know it was my position if I wanted it. The position would have to be announced. I was to go home and let First Sergeant and Commander know. At next month's drill I told them I was looking at going to OCS. Commander liked to talk. He said this would be good and we can promote some people giving them upper mobility. First Sergeant agreed it would be good for me, too. He said, "You know, Sergeant Humphrey, if you don't like OCS, you can always come home. There might not be a E7 slot available, though." I answered, "That's all right Sir. I have 27 years and can just go home and stay."

First Sergeant said I needed to tell the Admin NCO that I was looking to go to OCS, and I was going to transfer. The thing you have got to realize about the 2-263rd at that point in time was some of people were looking out for themselves. I was the only black E7, they wanted my transfer orders up that day. You cannot do that without the correct information. They did not have a paragraph line number or anything saying that I was going to OCS, but they did take my orders up that day.

Shortly after that we went to Fort Stewart, Georgia for summer camp. While at summer camp I told my First Sergeant and Commander, I needed to be at the Wet Site in Colombia for a class with the OCS. They gave me permission to go, gave me a Humvee, so I drove from Fort Stewart, Georgia to the Wet Site in Columbia, SC for the class. When I got back to Fort Stewart that Friday, by Saturday morning we were packing up ready to go home after the two week summer camp. I did not drill with Delta battery anymore after the two weeks of summer camp.

I transferred to Columbia, SC with the 218th Regiment as TAC NCO and I am very appreciative of my time with them. They really saw my worth and gave me a fair chance. They pointed out and recognized me for who I was and why I was there. As a black NCO, I did feel pressure indirectly and directly, but it made me a better soldier, man, and person. I had been overlooked for so long, even though I had the training and schooling required for certain positions.

I was there for five years and accomplished many things. I went through five classes at least and I know for sure some of the candidates that I was there with are now lieutenant colonels. One is getting ready to make a full bird colonel. The 218th Regiment was a lifesaver for me because they recognized my capabilities. Basically, as a black person and a TAC NCO under them, I had the same ability and the same authority as the officer TAC. If an officer were going too far, I could walk up to him and say, "Sir, back off." They respected me for who I was and for what I stood for.

At many summer camps, I would talk to the candidates at different units. Especially when we were in the field, I would give them my combat perspective and experience on what happened to me. I had that advantage over a lot of the officer TACs because none of them had been in combat. They respected my authority viewpoints and my opinion on whatever I had to say. It would be like, "If Sergeant Humphrey said it, then it's the gospel."

That was what my military career was in the 218th Regiment. I loved it and the people that I worked with. I wanted all the candidates to make the class. My advice to them was that they needed to show up and work hard for me to help them make it through. I would do whatever I could do to ensure that they made it through the process.

I had a lot of candidates that heeded my advice, and I helped them make it through. After five years, I got a call from the Admin NCO at OCS with the 218th Leadership. He told me that I was number one on the promotion board. They were looking at bringing a unit of ADA into Columbia which would be the 1-263rd. He told me that I needed to take that position. I told him I was happy doing what I was doing. Then he told me I would be crazy not to because it was going to be five to six years before they actually do anything. I took that position to get promoted and was promoted to E8 in 2000. I went over to the 1-263ʳᵈ Air Defense Artillery. I was the only black E8 in the 263ʳᵈ ADA.

There were people that I trained when they got to the National Guard as privates that made E8-first sergeants before I did. I was at the 1-263ʳᵈ and was First Sergeant to B-Battery. The only person I had in my battery was me so I would come to drill on Saturday mornings. I would ask the commander, Major Anthony Carson, what we had to do that day. He would say we do not have anything. I would tell him I would see him Sunday morning, get my little black hat, go back over to the OCS, and train the candidates. I did not do anything for about five or six years with the 1-263ʳᵈ.

I did the two week summer camp each year except for the one year OCS didn't have the money for me to attend Phase One. The OCS Commandant said that they had better find some money because I was a vital part of the OCS program and was going to be there. They found the money somewhere. I got to do the Phase One that year and I only missed one year because they did not have the money. I went over there anyway. The commander from the Florida unit told me if he had known that it was a money issue, he would have brought me on his budget and paid for it. So, I did the next time.

I was with the 1-263ʳᵈ for five years. We were unable to get enough people to form a battery. They disbanded the battery and took fifty of us to Kuwait under Operation Iraqi

Freedom to run a camp. The rest of the members were sent out to different companies and different units.

Preparing to go to Camp Arifjan in Kuwait, we started our training in Columbia, SC at our armory, and from there we went to North Carolina for more training. We deployed to Camp Arifjan in October 2004. I was the NCO IC of the ground crew which came up under the S4 section. Major Tim Webb was my boss. He later became Lieutenant Colonel when we got in country. We remained in Kuwait from October 2004 until October 2005.

During my deployment, I really enjoyed what we were doing. We had some obstacles that we had to overcome but I had the support of my immediate family. Others in the family were saying I did not need to go because I was too old. I was 57 years old and would turn fifty-eight in country. My wife and family really supported me. My wife Betty reminded them that they knew Harry the person, but she knew Harry the soldier, and I was going. My dad was blind, and my wife was taking care of him.

I realized before I left, that when I got back, I was gonna have about eighteen months before I turned sixty and retired. I went to the commander of the 218th regiment and told him that once I returned, I needed a position for at least eighteen months. He told me at that particular time, I could always come back to the 218th. I always had a home there. I had that in my pocket before I left for Kuwait.

We replaced the unit that was running the camp previously in Kuwait. We got to see a lot of units coming in and a lot of people going. We had Zone One, Zone Two and

Zone Six when we got there. We took down Zone Two and moved everybody over to Zone Six. We had to build a camp to accommodate the people that were coming from Zone Two. To get this done we had Third World country people working out on the base to do all the work.

My job was to make sure that we got things done. As the ground crew, we had the hardest job because we had to decommission tents, move equipment around, and do different things. I had some good men there working for me. In fact, I told them the workday was twelve hours a day, six days a week so when our job is over for the day, I'm not looking for anything to do. I had a good section with guys that worked for me that really enjoyed me. We had a great time and made friends with basically everybody that was at the camp.

When we got there, we had to do paperwork to requisition the trucks we needed, whether or not we may have got them or not. The camp was truckers because it was running convoys in and out of Camp Arifjan. When I needed trucks, after I got there, I learned who the Truckmasters were. I would go to the Truckmaster and most of the time I got what I needed. If forklifts were needed, I went down to the crane to the people that had the forklifts.

Zone One was interesting because it was paid for by the Kuwaitis who were rich. They had the money, so they put-up, and we were protecting them. The majority of the troops in Zone One were basically active duty troops.

Zone Six was paid for by the Americans. The reserve troops were in Zone Six. Zone One troops had hard instruction buildings, two men to a room, wireless internet, and little kitchenette between the rooms. The soldiers in Zone Six, where I was, had eight-men sleep tents. We had air conditioning and heat, so it wasn't that bad, but it was bad enough.

Zone One could not go to Zone Six to work or vice versa because they could not exchange the money. Zone One had a big PX, a full size gym with mirrors on the wall and any machine that you wanted to get into. It had a racquetball court, a basketball court, and an inground pool. It had a food court, but I cannot remember what was in their food court.

We finally got a gym, a PX, and got our food court built in Zone Six. In our food court was a Kentucky Fried Chicken, Hardee's, Charlie's Grill Sub, Subway, Starbucks coffee, and a Baskin Robbins ice cream shop. So, it really was a hard deployment there for a year. My Colonel said that I was the ambassador for Zone Six because I knew everybody there. I met and talked to everybody and had a good reputation among the people. There were a lot of Third World countries in Zone Six. A lot of stuff was brought in from the outside through the Third World countries.

We had some good times. I remember the Army's birthday. We celebrated it with a big dinner and a cake. One of my soldiers and I got to cut the cake because I was the oldest person in the theater, and he was the youngest. We had a big celebration for Christmas and Easter. I think the most wonderful thing about that deployment was whatever you did at home for religious service, you could also do that there. If you were on a dance team, a praise and worship team, sang in the choir, or played instruments at home, all that was available for you to do there. We had a really good religious group.

If you were a preacher, once your name got on the roster to preach, you were able to preach. I had to send papers home to request my license from my wife, so I could be put on the minister's rosters. If I preached on Friday, the next time I preached on Saturday. We had a Wednesday Bible Study, a Friday Joy night, a Saturday Night Live. With a Sunday morning service and a Sunday afternoon service, there was plenty to do there service-wise at Camp Arifjan. I only went off the camp twice and then I had to carry a weapon. The rest of the time we walked around the camp with no weapons, no flak jackets, no equipment, just our uniform and hat. We were in a good safe place and even had dinners and parties.

When I got in country, I was issued a 2004 Toyota Corolla and a cell phone. There was about an eight hour difference in time, so I was able to call home every night to talk to my wife or other family members.

All I had to do was lay up in my tent, call my office, my office would call the Armory, and the Armory would connect me to the house. We had a British camp there on base and when they came in for R & R, we took care of them. We got to be really good friends. They had a little break room, and we would go down to their break room a lot of times to talk, eat, and have fun with them. We had a good camp.

The difference between my deployment in Vietnam and Iraqi Freedom was that in Vietnam we were looking for the bad guys. In Iraqi Freedom there was not any of that going on and I was not out looking for the enemy. There were some troops out looking for the bad guys, but in my unit, we did not have to go outside the gate. We stayed on the inside and worked on the inside to run the camp. Another big difference was that we had better food than in Vietnam. In Vietnam we basically ate C-rations, but in Kuwait we had three to four meals a day. We had anything we wanted to eat: lobster tails, crab legs, T-bone steak, fish, salad bar, sandwich bar, and we had eggs to order every morning. We could go down to the food court and buy some food - a big difference from Vietnam.

We finished up our tour in Kuwait and got ready to come home. The commander, First Sergeant and S-1 had to find units for our group to go to when we got back home. My commander came to me and said, "Sergeant Humphrey, I don't think we'll be able to find a unit for you because you're an E8. I don't know what's out there for E8s?" I told him, "Sir, you don't have to worry about me. I'm going back to the 218th Leadership where I came from. I had that slot secured before we left the states." I am the person that learned to look out for themselves, and I looked out for my men while we were over there.

We demobilized in North Carolina when we got back from Kuwait. I went back to the 218th Regiment for my last year and a half. They slotted me with Fran Walters at OCS. Sergeant Drayton called me the Admin TAC. Basically, all I did was get up in the morning, pick up the candidates while the TACs got showers and got ready for class. I would give the TACs breaks in the classroom and harass the candidates; but I had no paperwork to do.

I retired from there in 2007 and came home. I was working at the Postal Service at that particular time. I rolled my time out until the very end, so that I did not have anything to do the last year and a half, while at the OCS besides show up and go to meetings.

The first few months out of service I missed my guys, my people and the candidates. Retirement was a big change and I still go back down there to visit. I go every year for Phase One. They know me now as the Legend. When I go, I get an opportunity to harass the candidates a little bit. I was inducted into the South Carolina Enlisted Hall of Fame on June 30, 2019. So, I am the Legend at OCS and that is what they call me when I go down there. I have really been blessed by the 218th Regiment. I have stayed in contact with some of the people that I served with like Fran, Drayton and Tim Webb.

I was awarded more than thirty military honors during my military career. A few of my awards and decorations include: Purple Heart Medal, Army Commendations Medal, 2 Army Achievement Medals, The Marine Combat Action Ribbon, Good Conduct Medal Army, Marine Corps Good Conduct Medal, Army Reserve Component Achievement Medal with One Silver Oak Leaf Cluster, three Bar Bronze Oak Leaf Clusters, 3 National Defense Service Medals, and others.

I learned a lot about myself in the military. Learned that I am able to do things that I thought I would never be able to do. It taught me to be a better leader, a better listener, and a better person, which really helped me as I went through life and the military. The military has greatly enriched my life.

For people that transition out of the military, I would advise them to find a veteran's group like Vets Helping Vets Anderson and join. Attend the meetings with other veterans that can actually help you in any situation that you need. When you talk to another veteran, they understand where you are at, what you have been through, and what you are doing.

I wish civilians understood that in the military services we are human just like everyone else. We went in to protect, to serve, and to keep them safe. I would do it again for anybody so they would not have to go through what I went through. We did not do it for ourselves but did it because we love our country, and we love people. I have a big word that I am famous for, I call people Hero.

My favorite phrases and words include the words of Lee Greenwood's song… *"I'm proud to be an American for at least I know I'm free and won't forget the men and women who died that gave that right to me."*
Then I turn that around and say, "I am proud to be a Christian for in Christ I know I'm free and I won't forget Jesus who died on Calvary."

I want my family to know that whatever I did, I did it for them. It was an honor to have served the United States military proudly for them. I appreciate everything that they did for me while I was away and after I got back home.

Vets Helping Vets means a lot to me. I can associate with the people that are talking about the things that they went through. I especially identify with the Monday night group, the PTSD group. It is the comradery.

We laugh and talk, pick at each other, and nobody gets mad. I use my testimony most of the time as a healing. It is healing for me to open up and be more transparent.

Once they had a PTSD group at the VA and then they cut it out. That really affected me because I was really being helped. Norm and a lot of my Campbell Patriot friends were trying to get me to come to VHVA, but I kept putting it off. Then my buddy Jeremiah Palmer was with the American Legion. Every time I saw him, he kept inviting me to join. Phil Harris kept urging me to join the Order of the Purple Heart.

I am part of Vets Helping Vets Anderson on Wednesday, the Monday night group, the Order of the Purple Heart, the Marine Corps League, and the American Legion Post 184, and the Campbell Patriots in which I am the commander. We do the military funerals for our veterans. Now I am a proud member of all these groups. I am more honored to be a soldier in God's Army.

Roy Ivey

My name is Roy R Ivey. I did not distinguish myself in high school though I did graduate in 1963 when I was nineteen. That summer, I left my mother in Milan and headed north on a solo bicycle ride through Italy, Switzerland, Germany, France, Luxemburg, Belgium, and England; twelve hundred miles in eleven days, without GPS, cell phone, or credit card. I had only a map and one hundred dollars.

I spent the next year in New Jersey, pumping gas and changing oil in a local garage. I also painted the Navy recruiter's house and guess what? Suddenly, I found myself in the Navy from 1964 until 1968. I maintain that I got far more out of the Navy than I put in.

After boot camp, I took Machinist's Mate Class A school, Basic Nuclear Power School, and Nuclear Submarine Prototype. Due to the loss of the Thresher (SSN-593) with one hundred twenty nine men in 1963, many of us "Nukes" were assigned to the non-nuclear surface fleet. As a MM2, I took two Mediterranean cruises and two Caribbean cruises on the USS Donner (LSD-20), a WWII 'gator freighter.

The giant bill paid most of my college tuition. I studied physics, had two engineering jobs, and in 1981 started CMA, a small business serving the paper converting industry.

Peggy and I are looking forward to an early retirement at the end of this year, when I will be 80 years old. We have three well launched kids. Susan is almost a Navy vet. She too has benefited from her service in the Navy. We have lived on Broadway Lake in Anderson South Carolina for more than twenty years, where we enjoy paddling our canoes. We support several local Anderson charities through our annual Friends of Broadway Lake Cardboard Boat Race. My membership in Vets Helping Vets heralds a new chapter. Peggy and I plan to do what we can for veterans who have given so much more than I ever did for our great country.

Note: I wrote this story of the Liberty Affair, which took place during the Six Day War. My story was chosen out of one hundred entries to be published in the Army ELITE Magazine.

"I Was There…Sort-Of"

"On June 8, 1967, then-President Lyndon Baines Johnson dishonored the thirty-four men killed and the 171 maimed, burned, and injured when their U.S. Navy ship, the USS Liberty was attacked by Israeli Air Force and Navy torpedo boats. Israel's Prime Minister Levi Eschkol asked Johnson to keep the incident quiet, and Johnson immediately issued an executive order that there was to be no investigation. To this day, no American politician has said or done anything to make sure the men of the USS Liberty would be honored or remembered."

So wrote Mr. Raymond Burgess of Central South Carolina in a letter to the editor of the Anderson S.C. newspaper, the Independent-Mail, several years ago. His letter brought tears to my eyes as I yelled for my wife. The stress in my voice caused her to rush in, perhaps fearing the worst.

I had told her about the Liberty affair but, until that day, I had never been able to prove the seemingly far-fetched story.

I admit to telling a few "Sea Stories" in my time, but this was not one of them.

On that day in 1967, I was a Second Class Machinist Mate aboard the USS Donner LSD-20 in the eastern Mediterranean. As a Machinist Mate, I was not aware of the overall mission of our ship or of the current events that were occurring around us. Somehow, however, I learned that the USS Liberty GTR-5 had been attacked and that several men had died.

My ship, the Donner pulled into Valletta Harbor, Malta a few days after the attack. The liberty had remained afloat but had been rendered dead-in-the-water by the attack and had to be towed to Valletta Harbor by the American carrier, USS Saratoga. After the Donner was moored in the harbor, and the Special Sea and Anchor Detail had been secured, I went over to the Liberty to check on a classmate named Morgan. Morgan and I were both graduates of the Nuclear Power Program, having been "trash-canned" to the surface fleet upon graduation from the S1C Prototype in Connecticut.

I was allowed to walk freely about the decks of the Liberty and to examine the many craters caused by the bombs and the torpedoes fired by the Israelis. I saw where seventeen men had died (later recorded as 34). Fortunately, my friend Morgan had been transferred off the Liberty weeks before the attack. I returned to my duties aboard the Donner and thought little more about the Liberty.

Upon my return stateside at the end of our Mediterranean cruise, I told my father about the Liberty and the fact that she was attacked by Israel. I could always tell when Dad thought I was off on another Fairy Tale or Sea Story. He looked over his glasses at me without saying a thing. One regret I have is that my father went to his grave before I had a chance to prove that this was no "Sea Story."

On looking back on the approximate timeline as I knew it, it seems that I went aboard the Liberty between three and six days after the attack. I think it took three days for the ship to be towed to Malta and about six days to lock down news of the attack, at the request of Israelis. If my timeline is more or less correct, it explains why I was allowed to roam freely about the decks and spaces and was never told to keep it under wraps. In fact, there is probably no record of my visit, other than the one indelibly etched into my memory. When I discovered the letter from Mr. Burgess in the paper, and after the few days required to regain my composure, I left a message on Mr. Burgess 's answering machine. I said I had read his letter and added, "I was there sort-of." I left my number and asked him to call me back. He did and we spoke several times. His story is very interesting.

Mr. Burgess was involved in intelligence gathering in Bremerhaven, Germany. Because the USS Liberty was also involved in this activity, there was a good communication between Liberty and Bremerhaven. Mr. Burgess was aware of the attack but was constrained by the President's executive order.

When the veil of secrecy was lifted, Mr. Burgess began a campaign to get the crew of the Liberty, all of whom were in harm's way, and thirty-four of whom had given their lives, honored for their service to our Great Country. I have not spoken to Mr. Burgess for several years, but I am sure he is still dedicated to that end. He should be commended for his efforts on behalf of those heroes aboard the USS Liberty GTR-5. The amazing story of the Israeli attack on the USS Liberty is detailed in chapter seven of the national bestseller, *Body of Secrets* by James Bamford, published by Anchor Books in 2001. **Roy R. Ivey**

Joe Kight

I was born in Clarkston near Stone Mountain, Georgia in 1935. Dad served in World War I as an Army medic. Otis and Paul, my two older brothers served in WWII. All my brothers, including Ben, served in the Navy. So, I thought as the youngest brother I would be different. I enlisted in the Marines in 1954 and did my basic at Parris Island, South Carolina. A giant Marine Sergeant stood behind me while I was filling out papers. He smacked me on the head and told me every line had to be filled out. I had left one blank because I was not given a middle name at birth. I promptly wrote Joseph Edward Kight, a made up name from then on for military purposes. I eventually got it straightened out and went back to my legal name, Joe Kight.

From there I was sent to Camp Pendleton in California for advanced infantry training. The training I endured there was mostly marching from desert to sea. This ensured we could be deployed, cover long distances and remain in top physical condition during combat. I was issued a Browning Automatic Rifle (BAR) with a magazine that held twenty rounds. I was deployed and got as far as Japan. We got word that they were negotiating. With Vietnam unstable, we stayed in the Pacific area to be ready to go wherever we were needed.

I received orders to report to Hawaii and was to be stationed at Kaneohe. I smelled the sweet aroma of flowers as the ship got closer to the Island. The Pali Pass in the mountains of the Northeastern part of Oahu was an ideal training site for maneuvers. I was in a Heavy Mortar Unit. When my service time was up, I was sent to the San Francisco

Bay area to process out. This was 1959. I headed back to Georgia and remained a year in a reserve unit driving a truck.

After gluing labels on metal cans for a while, a friend enticed me into using my G.I. Bill and attend the University of Georgia with him. I received a bachelor's degree in forestry and wildlife Management and then a master's degree in wildlife biology. I met my lovely wife Glenda at the university. She received a master's in food technology. We have been married for over sixty-two years. We have a son and daughter, six grandchildren, 1great grandchild, and one on the way.

I worked in Georgia, Texas, Alabama, Virginia. Tennessee, and retired from the Corp of Engineer as an Aquatic Plant Biologist at Lake Seminole, Florida. While working as a wildlife biologist, I won the Wildlife Biologist of the Year award for Alabama.

My hobbies were many. I became interested in muzzleloaders and decided to build my on replica 45 caliber. I joined an organized club and started competitive shooting. I won a trophy in Mississippi for best marksmanship for the year using the muzzleloading rifle I made. For part of the rifle, I used the metal from the runner of a sleigh. I loved assembling model airplanes, seeing the motorized ones fly, and winning awards for my models. My son and I spent his growing up years doing this together. I would encourage parents today to find hobbies to share with your children. These hobbies can lead to exciting and successful lives. My son built three planes of his own and participated in flying aerobatic shows throughout the world. He presently works as a corporate project engineer for Shaw Industries.

I have many interesting stories of survival and wrote some of them down to share: *I'd like to tell you about two of them and how Angels have affected my life. There have been quite a few times when they have interceded on my behalf; on the ground, in and on the water, and in the air. Pastor told me about a book written by Billy Graham, Angels, God's Secret Agents, published in 1975 that sold over three million copies. It says the Bible has over four hundred references about Angels.*

As a kid I used to wonder about angels. Most of the pictures of Angels that I saw were of naked babies with little bitty wings, usually blowing a horn. Didn't seem like wings that small could lift a big fat baby. But then a bumblebee has a big body and relatively small wings and it seemed to do all right. So, I figured it was another one of God's wonders and let it go at that.

Since I became an adult, by legal definition, anyway, (Grand-mama doesn't think I ever really grew up) I have come to believe that there is no such thing as coincidence or 'luck.' I think everything happens for a reason and that Angels play a major role in those happenings. This feeling has been developing over a long span of time. You've all heard the expression, 'boy that was a stroke of luck!' when something fortunate happened. Well, too many things have happened to me to think that they 'just happened.' I don't believe in 'coincidences' either.

I believe that I have a guardian Angel. Sometimes I think there must be a whole squadron of them to have been able to pull me out of some of the messes I've gotten into. This was really brought to a head back in the early 1970s. I had been vaguely aware that something was going on before that but wasn't really clear on just what it was.

I was working for the US Forest Service in Texas at the time, doing a wildlife habitat survey in the Big Thicket area in East Texas. This involved dividing some 633,00 plus acres into compartments of two to four thousand acres of similar habitat, making a map, establishing compass lines on that map and then walking the lines, cataloging conditions and making notes of possible improvements. On this particular day I was surveying a compartment on the backside of way yonder. Drove to the end of an old logging road. And then walked a mile or two to get to the start of my first compass line. After a while, the line came into a small creek. It had a hard sandy shallow bottom, but the banks were very steep and about four to five feet high. I walked downstream for a couple hundred feet and couldn't find a crossing. Went back upstream about the same length and still couldn't find a low place in the bank. So, I went back to where I first came to the creek and decided to just slide on down the bank and get dirty climbing up the other side.

About that time, I felt a very gentle force leading me away from where I was going to jump off. I moved over a few feet and stepped off, digging my heels in and sliding down the bank. Made it O.K. and took a step or two to regain my balance and then turned around to look back at the bank

152

where I had slid down. This was in the summertime, very hot, humid and not a breath of air stirring. I broke a cold sweat anyway. There, about five feet on each side of my 'slide' tracks were two cottonmouth moccasins coiled up in little niches in the bank. They were three to four feet long with bodies as big around as my arm. And I slid down exactly halfway between them. If I had slid down the bank where I started to or four or five feet either up or down stream, I would have slid right over the top of either one or the other. Considering the heat and how far it was back to the truck, and with no radio, I would have been in big trouble.

Question is, how did I know where to slide down that bank? Answer is, I DIDN'T KNOW! I was led. I was being looked after and cared for. This really convinced me. I could go on with several close call snake stories but most folks, including me, don't like snakes. So, I'll move on to another example of Angels in action.

A few years later, I was in charge of trying to manage aquatic vegetation in Lake Seminole in Georgia, Florida and Alabama. We, the pilot and I, were flying up the lake in an UH 4B helicopter (that's like the ones that were used so much in Vietnam) to check out an operational site. It was early morning, absolute calm, fog over the water, sun not up on the lake yet. Surface like a mirror, reflecting the mist. Pilot got spatially disoriented, and we hit the water going about 100 mph. Totally demolished the helicopter. Luckily, (there's that word again) when everything had stopped moving, (First break) the cabin was in a more or less upright position.

153

(Second break) I was still mostly conscious, (Third break) I was able to take a deep breath before the cabin sank.

Then it got kinda hairy. The thing sank like a rock, and I couldn't find the seat harness release. The Huey was a former Army and had really good (big and wide) harness straps (shoulder straps and seat belts). The deeper I sank, the darker it got until it finally was as dark as I had ever experienced. I had a feeling of disappointment, knowing that I wasn't going to get out of this one.

All this time, I had been hooking my left thumbs under the shoulder straps and following them down to the lap belt. Between the shoulder straps and the lap belt was where the release buckle was supposed to be. But it wasn't there. Just more belt webbing. I was running out of air and involuntarily inhaled a tiny bit of water. My respiratory system just shut down. I couldn't have inhaled if I wanted to. By this time, I was on the bottom of the lake under 20 feet of water, still strapped to the wreckage.

Then a very short clip of a movie flashed through my mind. Have you seen the movie, <u>An Officer And A Gentleman</u>? It's about this guy going through Navy pilot training. He was strapped in a seat, run down the slide into a pool of water, winding upside down. Object of the exercise was to let out a couple bubbles to see which way is up, release the harness and follow the bubbles. As this went through my mind, I realized the release buckle was not in the middle but was on my left hip! I reached over, hit the release, and then was in the mud on the bottom of the lake clear of the wreckage. Later on, looking at the salvage wreckage, I didn't see any way to have gotten clear of all that mess of broken twisted aluminum. But there I was. And, being possessed of a sharp, scientific mind, I figured that if I was on the bottom, then the surface was probably in the other direction. So, I pushed off the mud with both legs. That's when I discovered that my right leg was shattered just below the knee. Inhaled another little sip of water, drifted, floated to the surface. Couldn't swim very well as body parts wouldn't do what my mind told them to do. Didn't know about the three broken ribs on my left side. Bother... Finally made it to the surface and got a lung full of fresh air. A pretty girl's perfume was never as sweet.

The tail boom had broken off just back of the cabin and was still afloat. The pilot, who was not hurt very badly, towed me over to it. He had already made two dives trying to find me. Then after three or four deep breaths, the boom sank. We looked around and there was nothing left floating that was bigger than our fist. Well, here we go again and after all that! But my Angel came through again. Up pop the seat cushion! Not a flotation device, just a canvas covered foam rubber seat cushion. But it floated. We latched on to that and were able to make our way to a wood piling that marked the boat channel. By then the seat cushion had become waterlogged and was barely floating. We were able to take our belts off, hook them together, and tie them around the piling. We were able to hold on until a man and his wife rescued us. The man pulled up the lake from us and proceeded to throw out the anchor, arrange things in his boat, get his wife all rigged up, and finally settled down to fish. They were just within shouting distance so after they settled down and quit making so much racket, we started

155

hollering at them. Then, seems there was another small problem. The man was hard of hearing!

Wife: 'Do you hear somebody hollering?'

Man: 'No.'

Wife: 'There's somebody hollering over that way.' She points in our direction.

Man: 'It's probably just some kids. There's a swimming area over that way.'

Wife: 'No, I don't think so. I think somebody's in trouble. Let's go see.'

So, they did and bless her heart. The pilot had on a white shirt and was able to take it off and wave with it. They came over and pulled up beside us. The pilot stepped up on the lower unit of the outboard and got in the skiff boat with no trouble. I went headfirst over the side which was an experience. Broken leg, ribs and all. All this happened in a very timely manner as I was going deeper in shock!

Finally got to the hospital and 'lucked out' again. My Angel was on overtime by now but came through once more. The surgeon on call was a bone specialist. A day or so later, after I was more or less stable, he came by the room with X-rays of my leg and gave me three options:

1. *They could open it up and try to get everything back in order. On the X-ray, I counted eight pieces of bone about the size of one joint of your finger.*
2. *They could give it a couple days and see what happened.*
3. *Last resort, Amputation. I voted for number two, and he agreed. Found out later that the other*

surgeon who happened to be off that day would have opened it up. Much more complicated and dangerous due to possible infection. Plus, more things to heal.

Turned out it was the right thing to do. After several days in the hospital, they changed
cast three times in three days; I received assorted therapy (those people are sadists), learned to walk again, and everything returned to pretty much normal.

I checked out a Cessna 172, flew it up and down, over several rivers, and over Okefenokee Swamp. Sort of a 'get back on the horse that threw you' kind of thing. Must have worked because I still enjoy flying and have had only one bad dream about the whole thing.

And my Angel(s) are still on the job. And as an aside, back when the Huey helicopter was being developed, there were several fatalities due, as later discovered, to faulty seat design. The powers that be, assigned the problem to the Navy Safety Center at NAS Norfolk, Virginia and told them to fix it. After much redesign and testing, they fixed the problem. The seat, and hopefully anyone in it, could survive a major mishap. The seat I was in was the result of the Navy Safety Center's work. One of the leaders of the team that developed the new seat was a guy named Lieutenant Commander Otis Kight. HE'S MY BROTHER!. Coincidence?

My older brother, Lieutenant Commander Otis Kight, served the aircraft carrier USS Yorktown (CV-5) at the battle of Coral Sea and Midway. He was only seventeen. He joined the U.S. Navy on his seventeenth birthday, July 29,1941. One month after graduating Clarkston High School in Georgia, where I later graduated in 1953. Otis retired after thirty years, and also served during the Korean and Vietnam Wars. My brother minced no words and is quoted as saying: *All of us on the Yorktown in '42 were of 'The Depression' era. Life and death were accepted as part of the ongoing history, without heart bypass, miracle 'silver Bullet' antibiotics, hip replacements and things we take as normal now. People got sick; they died. People who lived past sixty-five were 'old people.' Death did not have the horror or shock it does to the last two or three generations. If we had another Desert Storm, and we (the US) lost two thousand troops in five hours, the country would have a cow. Between Pearl Harbor and Tarawa, we lost twice that many and didn't even draw in a deep breath.*

My brother is also quoted as saying to a group speaking of his fellow Americans who died defending at Coral Sea and Midway: *Those people gave up their today so we could have our tomorrow. This is that tomorrow! So, enjoy the hell out of it, and live for the thousands or so people that died for us to have it.* Wise words from my brother that the youth of today need to understand. The freedoms they enjoy are not free. Many sacrificed their lives for the America they loved.

After moving sixteen times while working in the wildlife management field, we moved to Anderson, South Carolina in 2000 to be near our son, daughter and grandchildren. Our daughter has an Elementary Education degree and spent many years as a librarian. We are active in the Varennes Heights Baptist Church. My wife sings in the choir and plays the flute in the church orchestra. She says I am the most honest person that she has ever met, and she loves my sense of humor. Friends Scotty Murdock and Dusty Holmes invited me to Vets Helping Vets Anderson. I enjoy the camaraderie with my friends there.

Ed King

I was born twelve days after the attack on Pearl Harbor in the home of my aunt and uncle on Route 1, Piedmont, South Carolina. We raised cows, chickens, pigs, turkeys, and a garden to feed us. We also had cotton, tobacco, and pigs. My father owned a self-propelled combine and a truck for support of this machine in the 1950s. I was trained to operate both. In other words, I was raised to WORK!

Attending the White Plains School, I graduated in the second class from Wren High School in Piedmont in May 1959. Enrolling in Clemson College, I began my adult life? I learned how to play bridge, hitchhike, and the important things in life. I worked with an electrical contractor building the Dunlop Golf Ball plant in Westminster, South Carolina during the summer between my second and third semester at Clemson College.

I joined the United States Army in February 1961 after three semesters at Clemson. Wasting my own money last semester. I felt the best thing for me was the military, and I was bussed to Fort Jackson, Columbia, South Carolina for two Zero weeks. Then I went to Fort Benning, Georgia for two more weeks before beginning (BCT) Basic Combat Training.

Upon completion of basic, I was trained for 81mm mortar platoon and the fire direction center. We continued with further unit training as an infantry company and then trained as a division in maneuvers at Fort Benning - 2nd Infantry Division. The Berlin crisis froze all transfers, so I was in training and some type of maneuvers, until the cool down of the crisis.

Then I received orders to the United States Army in Alaska and reported in September 1962. While on leave, before going to Alaska, my mother convinced me to date Miss Barbara Ridgeway, my future wife. We had three dates before I left. I had no idea how much those dates would affect my future. On the way to Alaska, I visited the World's Fair in Seattle, Washington. And call Barbara! Then flew to Alaska.

I was assigned to the 4.2 inch mortar platoon and the fire direction center. We trained for all types of weather, and they held maneuvers with units from the lower forty-eight states. I saw some very cold weather!! I had reached the rank of Specialist 5 and served part time as company clerk, among other duties. I entered the Noncommissioned Officer (NCO) academy and was promoted to Sergeant. (Also, reenlisted while in the field in December 1963.)

After writing many letters and a few $7 per three-minute phone calls, I returned to South Carolina with a diamond in my pocket and married my sweetheart! I returned to Alaska with her on my arm in January 1964. We went through the 9.2 earthquake on March 27, 1964. It was quite an experience. She stood by during the many alerts and training exercises in Alaska.

I was transferred to Fort Jackson, SC in September 1965 and given a position as training aid NCO for the Training Brigade. This went well until someone realized I was drawing proficiency pay as a mortar soldier. My name came down in December for Vietnam. The brigade commander contacted me and recommended I go to Officer Candidate School. I was processed in two days, and the paperwork was forwarded to my shipment back to Fort Benning, Georgia.

Reported to Officer Candidate Class 110-66 to begin training. I was commissioned as a Second Lieutenant on June 30, 1966, assigned to be an instructor on the 81mm mortar at the United States Army Infantry School. Remaining there through April 1967 until I was assigned to a packet group at Fort Lewis, Washington. I served as a platoon leader for a Construction Engineer Platoon for a month and then we trained our troops for duty in Vietnam.

In July 1967 we boarded the USS Geiger and spent twenty-one days in transit to Vietnam. We did not make an overnight stop in Guam on the way. I was assigned to the 1st Infantry Division, THE BIG RED ONE, and in Phuoc Vinh, and after reporting for duty was assigned to lead an 81mm mortar platoon. After a few weeks and several operations, the Battalion Commander told me to provide him with a Table of Organization and Equipment (TO&E) to support the Battalion's four rifle companies. I came up with eight guns and sixty-five men. This was approved and I led this group until being assigned as XO of Headquarters Company.

Two weeks before my date to rotate back to the United States, I was sent back to the field to lead the mortar platoon again. Scary times! During my service in Vietnam, I was responsible for approximately 10,000 mortar rounds being fired. We actually sank two sampans (boats) going down river.

I returned to the United State and was again assigned to the Weapons Department at the Infantry School as an instructor on the Small Arms Committee. I was reassigned to the Department Headquarters two months before separation as Admin Officer. This meant I signed my name over and over for two months. I left the service on June 30, 1969.

I would have loved to make a career in the Army, but I could not take the extreme heat in Vietnam. I sweat so badly that I cannot replace the water as fast as I lose it. I worked in the shop at a cotton mill for about six weeks before deciding to move to something with more future. Then I worked as a customer service man with Simplex Time Recorder Company for about six years. Feeling led to move on, I went to work for the Greater Greenville Sanitation as a route supervisor and then as a maintenance manager. This led to my retirement.

The summer of 2022, I met a veteran at the Anderson Jockey Lot. He led me to Mr. Crawford who gave me a Vets Helping Vets Anderson card and invited me to attend a meeting. A few weeks later, my wife and I did go to a meeting and the rest is history. A fantastic group with much in common and Amens along the way!! The highlight of our week, other than church, is attending these meetings. Thanks all of you for the warm welcome!

In Memory of
Adam Charles Kocheran
(1972-2003)

Adam was a native of Columbus, Ohio, graduated the United States Military Academy in June 1993 and was commissioned a Second Lieutenant in the infantry. His initial assignment was an Infantry Rifle Platoon Leader in Bravo Company, 3rd Battalion, 22nd Infantry Regiment, 25th Infantry Division (Light) from July 1994 to February 1996. CPT Kocheran was then assigned to Bravo Company 1st Battalion, 75th Ranger Regiment, serving as a Rifle Platoon Leader and Support Platoon Leader from March 1996 to May 1998. CPT Kocheran's branch transferred to Special Forces upon completion of the Special Forces Qualification Course in 1998.

From 1999 to July 2001, CPT Kocheran served as a Commander of SFOD-A 714 (Military Free Fall) in Company A 1st Battalion, 7th Special Forces Group (Airborne); from August 2001 to December 2002, he served as commander of SFOD-A (assault) in Company C, 3rd Battalion, 7th Special Forces Group (Airborne) and 01 January 2003 to 26 January 2003 served as Commander of SFOD-A 796 (Sniper/Observer) Company C, 3rd Battalion, 7th SFG (Airborne).

CPT Kocheran's awards and decoration included the Meritorious Service Medal, Army Commendation Medal (with 2 Oak Leaf Clusters) Army Achievement Medal (with 1 Oak Leaf Cluster) National Defense Service Medal, Overseas

Medal, Expert Infantryman's Badge, the Master Parachutist's Badge, the Military Free Fall Jumpmaster Badge, Ranger Tab, Special Forces Tab, German Parachutist's Badge, Chilean Carabinero Parachutist's Badge and Colombian Expert Parachutist's Badge.

Adam was one of three Special Forces troops hurt by a Claymore mine blast during routine training exercises at Camp Santiago in southeastern Puerto Rico. A serious head wound left him brain dead and his family chose to remove him from life support. The other two troops were treated and released.

On the day of land-mine accident that took his life, CPT Kocheran turned to his fellow soldiers and said: "Can you believe we get paid to do this: I love doing what I'm doing."

Adam, an April Fool's Day baby, wore many hats and could be quite the comedian. Adam attended a church service with Aunt Penny and Uncle Dave. It was "hat day" at the church. When Aunt Penny looked out into the congregation from the choir loft, Adam, who was more accustomed to wearing a black beret was donning a big blue ladies' hat and a smile. He was a friend who entertained his buddies – and a bachelorette party – with an impromptu strip tease at a bar, who in his spare time taught a friend's wife to speak Spanish, one of four foreign languages that he spoke.

Adam was a driven, focused and competitive man. A solid man who took his career seriously. On February 8, 2003, hundreds of family and friends gathered to mourn and recall a life that despite its short duration included innumerable achievements and memorable encounters. At the front of the church, Adam's Green Beret hung from his rifle, his shiny black boots close by. Adam was 31 years old.

NOTE: Adam was the nephew of Penny Kocheran Davis. Penny is a member of VHVA Wives and wife of David Davis, member of Vets Helping Vets Anderson.

Barbara Kulusic

My name is Barbara Pirylis Kulusic. I grew up in New Jersey as the fourth child out of six children. When I was two, my mom contracted tuberculosis. My older brothers Ed and Don, my sister "Leenie" and I all tested positive, but it was not active like Mom's. I was placed in a hospital for children because I was younger. My older siblings got to stay home. We lived in the apartment building owned by my grandparents. Other relatives lived in the apartment building, also. They helped my dad watch my brothers and sister.

Behind the apartment was a bakery my grandparents owned. My dad and his brothers worked at the bakery before World War II. After Pearl Harbor, Hawaii was attacked, my uncle Nuddy enlisted to fight for the United States. After he experienced Operation Torch, the allied invasion of French North Africa against the Nazi's, he wrote home telling his brothers not to join the Army. If they did, he would come back and kill them himself. They all went into the Navy.

My dad and his brother served in the Atlantic and then the Pacific against Japanese Imperialism. Dad was a Signal man. You had to be proficient in map reading, morse code, and visual communication with flags and lights. One day a Kamikaze (suicidal) plane bombed an American ammunition ship and the concussion of the blast knocked Dad off the conning tower of his ship. The plane was shot down before crashing into his ship. He ended up working in the Officer's mess while recuperating since he was such a good baker. So, the moral of the story is: it does not matter where you fought, WAR SUCKS! They all came home after the war "scarred" which was the term they used back then, not PTSD.

In 1960, when I was five years old, I came home from the hospital. Then there were five of us since my brother John was born while I was in the Children's Hospital. A few months later we moved into a bigger house. The next year my sister Nancy was born. Growing up in the sixties my mom stayed home with the kids while my dad worked. This was how most families were back then. My grandma came to live with us after grandpa died, then my Nana. We constantly had lots of relatives visiting.

I went to Catholic school where we had nuns as teachers. Some of them had no patience with children. When I was in the third grade Friday November 22, 1963, President Kennedy was shot. We all were sent home. The following Monday, we had the day off to watch the funeral on TV. Three days later was Thanksgiving Day. It was more sober than thankful. One day when I was in the sixth grade my mom had enough of the abuse from the nuns. She pulled my older brother, sister, and myself out of the Catholic school and enrolled us in public school. What a culture shock that was for me as a twelve-year old! There was more diversity and culture, less rules and regulations.

Summers were fun for us kids. We would ride our bikes, roller skate, walk around the neighborhood, or take the bus downtown to shop. My closest friends were Mary and Gae. All of us would go to the Boylan Street pool to swim, then to the lemon ice stand on the way back home. At "Bradley Court" apartments, down the street from where I lived, we could play basketball, softball, and ping pong outside. We would sit and talk while we waited for our turn to play. Afterwards, we would go to Ziegler's Soda Shoppe, or Pat and Ann's Pizzeria. Another favorite place within walking distance was the Stanley Movie Theater, where you could see movies (flicks) for only twenty-five cents. I remember seeing *A Hard Day's Night* that starred The Beatles there. We would go to Elmwood or Vailsburg Park and play on the swings or on an airplane that was in the middle of the park. It had been gutted. We could climb in and all over it, jumping off the wings, and out the doors like we were wearing parachutes. Was this an omen to what I would do in the future in my Naval service as a parachute rigger (PR)?

Camp counselors kept us busy doing crafts and playing games. The tennis courts were used a lot in the summer. In the winter they would be filled with water so we could go ice skating. When we got cold we would walk in our skates over to the huge barrel full of burning wood and would sit around it to warm up. One year a man gave my dad a big box full of comic books, so we could sit outside with our friends and read them all summer! I try not to think of how much those old comic books would sell for now. Most of the neighbors knew each other and looked out for all of us kids. If we were doing something wrong or right it wasn't unusual for them to "call us out" and then call our folks. I worked shoveling snow, raking leaves, babysitting, and later at the ice cream parlor, and as a salesclerk in a drug store.

My sister Leenie and I shared a room, laughs, cigarettes, and clothes. One winter evening, she and her friends took me to the corner phone booth by Reiley's Tavern and pierced my ears! We walked to the food fair to grocery shop with mom, pulling the cart. You could fit four large paper bags full of groceries in that cart. It was great exercise, but we did it because it was one of our expected chores. Our uncle Frank finished his time honorably in the Marine Corps. He gave my older brother Ed his blue Corvair, to drive us home on hot or rainy days.

In April 1968, Martin Luther king was shot, and two months later Robert Kennedy was also assassinated. There were so many racial riots in Newark, New Jersey, and the big cities throughout the country. I remember hearing gunshots, something we were not used to in my town. During high school, we would "hang out" at Karen's house and go to concerts, Seaside Heights, local diners, or to the South Mountain Reservation to hike the waterfalls. We would listened to music played by local musicians, or someone's transistor radio powered by nine volt batteries. Many of the tunes were Motown, Doo-Wop, and Folk songs about peace and ending the Vietnam war. Kids my age did not know much about the war, except for what we overheard from our families and Walter Cronkite. I did not know anyone personally that served in Vietnam. We did not think badly about those in the military, because we had too many of our families that had served in the past. We were proud of them all.

From 1971 to 1973, there were many changes for me. I went to a new high school, my sister got married, and my younger brother got beat up badly by three guys who stole his papers and paper route money. That was the last straw for my parents! There were three kids at home by then. They sold our home in East Orange and moved us to a safer town. I did not like it at first. It was too country for me with wild animals and no sidewalks!

One night my mom and dad went out leaving me home with my younger brother John, sister Nancy, and our dog Frisco. We let Frisco out in the yard and the next thing we knew was his barking turned to crying. He had gotten sprayed by one of the wild animals, a skunk! I had read somewhere that tomatoes help take away the smell. We took everything we could find in the house that had tomatoes in it: ketchup, canned tomatoes, fresh tomatoes, and tomato juice. We squeezed, poured, and smashed it all over him in the front yard. While we were in the process of doing this, my parents came home. What a sight that must have been!

I got a job at Rockaway Sales, in the record department as a salesclerk, cashier and DJ. It was such a fun job, and I worked with wonderful people. My brother Don joined the Navy as a corpsman in the mid 70's. I visited him and his family at different bases like Camp Lejeune, North Carolina and NAS Key West. This was my first inkling of what military life was like. In 1981, I was serving on the New Jersey Grand Jury, for a one year obligation. My friends were getting married and having babies. I was in an abusive relationship, so I joined the Navy in the delayed entry program. It was hard to leave my friends and family, my nephews especially. My father was worried yet proud of me at the same time. He told me to watch out for those sailors! I was allowed to leave the grand jury duty because of my military obligation.

In December of 1981, I went to boot camp in Orlando, Florida. I was in KO33. I overcame fears and gained confidence with the help from my fellow recruits. Our days were filled with classes, marching, getting yelled at, getting shots, learning how to get along, and working together as a team. You could smoke back then in boot camp, so at the end of the day that was an escape of sorts.

Swimming was not a strong point for me. I was afraid of heights. We had to climb to the top of the high dive, in our clothes, to simulate abandoning ship. Then we were supposed to thread water to the side of the pool. I let my fellow recruits go ahead of me, till I was last in line. I climbed that ladder, then froze when I got to the top. I could not bring myself to go out to the diving board. My CC PO1 Jones was yelling at me to jump. It took her climbing to the top of the ladder and threatening to push me, for me to take the plunge! That was it for me, I did it, I survived.

My family was great about sending me letters to remind me I was cared about. My brother Ed and sister-in-law Susan sent a box of homemade cookies, enough for the whole company. We got in trouble the day the cookies arrived, so we did not get to eat them until a few days later. They sure tasted great! After graduation I was in great shape physically. I went to Parachute Rigor, a school in Lakehurst, New Jersey. One of my roommates had a huge tattoo of a Jimmy Hendrix album cover on her back. That was the first time I had ever seen a girl with a tattoo. I learned how to inspect survival equipment, pack parachutes and inflatables, and sew. For weeks we had to jump off a platform to simulate parachute landing falls (PLF's). Those practice jumps served to make a boot camp's foot injury worse. On PR graduation day, I was not allowed to jump with my classmates. I am not sure to this day if I was angry or relieved!

My first duty station was in Pensacola Florida at Aircraft Intermediate Maintenance Department (AIMD). We were located in the same hangar with the Navy/ Marine Corps Blue Angels. Formed in 1946, the unit is the second oldest formal acrobatic team in the world. It was thrilling to watch them practice for air shows, especially with visitors from Canada and Britain. Our commanding officer, Captain JB McKamey had been a prisoner of war (POW) in Vietnam for eight years. He was a great man and leader.

I met my future husband, Joe a Machine Repairman (MR) at AIMD. I was still a smoker when we started dating. He said that he could not kiss me with that cigarette breath. I credit him for being the major reason I quit and for giving me my first Bible. We married in 1984. When he was transferred to sea duty to Mayport, Florida, I was given spouse orders to Helicopter Squadron (HS-1), NAS Jacksonville.

I got pregnant a few months later. I felt great physically during my pregnancy and excited for our child to arrive. When John was born, we learned much about early parenting from our friends in the Navy, and the "Navigators" with Ren and Birgitta Zepp.

I did not reenlist for another tour at that time, because my husband was going to be working in the family business in Michigan where my in-laws lived. My mother and father-in-law were very instrumental in helping us learn more about the love of Jesus, and His love of us. I joined the Reserves at Naval Air Facility (NAF), Detroit, at Selfridge Air National Guard Base (SANG), VP-93 (Executors), working in the PR shop and on "the line" where I was a "wing walker," "brake rider," and would also launch and recover aircraft (A/C).

I took a few spills on the Michigan ice that I physically deal with to this day. We went on deployments to Roda, Spain for two weeks active duty service each year. The history and the architecture was amazing! I went back on active duty and transferred to VR-62, also at NAF Detroit. They flew the C9B Skytrain II.

As an enlisted, lower ranked person, walking the watch was a normal thing before moving up to the Quarterdeck, manning the phones and being the contact center between the enlisted and Commanding or Executive Officers. I had some interesting watches. One Sunday in the new VR-62 hangar in Detroit, the new fire extinguishing system inadvertently went off. The hangar was full of foam. The duty section was not happy to have to come in and clean that up. During another watch at night, I had a young sailor, a mom-to-be, show up in labor. I was tasked to be a pallbearer at the funeral of a fellow sailor. It was a very solemn moment in my life. It was cold but we all did our best to honor her family by letting them know how important she was to a fellow military member.

I went to instructor school for (9502) in Great Lakes, Illinois. In February and March of 1993, Brrrr. I qualified as a sharpshooter on the M16 in 1993, the only time I shot it.

Due to Base Realignment and Closure (BRAC), NAF Detroit was closed, and the squadron was moved to Naval Air Station (NAS), South Weymouth. VR-62 nomads, transitioned to C130's before arriving there in 1994. I was excited about moving there, since it would be closer to my family in New Jersey. My dad passed away a few months before we moved there. We bought a Cape Cod house in Carver, Massachusetts that my husband, my brother (mainly), my nephew, and son helped to renovate. A few sailors from my squadron, bribed by food, helped us, too. We loved it there! Hiking, skiing, and the history were so wonderful to be around. We were there for two years before BRAC shut down NAS South Weymouth, also. That closure put a huge strain on many families, including mine.

While my husband and son stayed behind in November 1996, I was transferred to VP-92 (Minuteman) at NAS Brunswick, Maine. I was working on the line again as a "wing walker," "brake-rider," and would launch and recover A/C before going to the PR shop, then (TAD) Temporary Assigned Duty to the AIMD there. Less than three years later, while the base was slowly shutting down, I was up for orders again in July of 1999. I transferred to NAF Washington D.C. to the Reserve AIMD (RAIMD). Only my son came with me.

I was also a CPR instructor and worked in quality assurance. I was promoted to E6 and just like most who got a promotion, (wherever you were stationed) you went through a type of "ceremony." Ours consisted of getting taped to a chair on wheels. The lucky ones did not end up under the wash station for a shower while in uniform. I was lucky that time.

Understand, it was not a bad thing to happen. Everywhere I was stationed, most of the military members were away from their families. Commands would make an extra effort to have a holiday meal for the Sailors and Marines. Usually, fryers were set up outside the hangar. They would cook a bunch of turkeys and tables would fill part of the hangar. Everyone would pitch in for the rest of the meal. There was enough food to feed everyone. We would also have a family picnic in the summer.

A tornado came through LaPlata, Maryland causing a lot of damage. All the commands at Andrew Air Force Base were scheduled to go there for weeks to help with the cleanup. We were cutting up felled trees, removing debris, setting up food and coffee distributions, locating veterans who were eligible for some type of aid, etc.

The medals and ribbons I am most proud of are the ones I received with the rest of the units I was stationed with at different times. We worked as a team and accomplished our goals. Awards: Good Conduct Medal 5(1986, 1990, 1994, 1999); Armed Forces Reserve Medal 1 (87 through 97); Joint Meritorious Unit Award (97); Battle "E" (98); Coast Guard Spec Ops Service Ribbon (87); National Defense Service Medal (90).

I retired from there in October 2004 as a PR1/E6. I missed the people and the teamwork when I left, and the paycheck. Freedom is a word that means so much more to me since serving. Knowing how many people around the world do not have it. How many times my family and many others fought for freedom, so that we can keep the rights that are in the United States Constitution and the Declaration of Independence.

One of the things I would want my family to know is that I am sorry for all the disruptions and sacrifices in their lives, due to the multiple transfers from base closures and decommissioning's. Congress did not take into account how many lives would be affected negatively by their actions.

I went to Cosmetology school and graduated in 2006. I worked in the Unique Chic salon for a few years. I moved back to New Jersey to help my brothers and sister with my mom who was still ill. It was great to be able to spend time with my family again.

After a few years I moved to South Carolina with my son and grand dog, Max. I found a great church and met some people at a veteran's event of Vets Helping Vets Anderson. I joined after attending a few meetings. We have a veteran from World War II, a few from the Korean War and many from the Vietnam War. There are new ones coming in who served in war and conflicts in Iraq, Afghanistan, and multiple other countries around the world. We have a growing number of members including other female veterans. I am the librarian for our small contingent of books and videos that have been donated by our members. Hopefully, we will be in our new building by 2024, so that we can have more veterans come, enjoy, and feel like a member of our family, too!

I have two pieces of advice about going into the military. If you need direction and at the same time want to experience life and be a part of something bigger than yourself, join soon after high school. If you can wait a couple years, get your associate degree in a community college. Learn American and world history. Volunteer locally. Take advantage of seeing everywhere you can, wherever you are because you may not ever be there again. Stay connected with the people whom you developed a friendship with. These relationships are important.

Ronnie McMahan

My name is James Ronald McMahan, but most call me Ronnie Mac and this is my story. I am the eldest child of four children to Reese and Elizabeth McMahan of Iva South Carolina. I was born and raised on the Jackson Mill Hill in Iva, and I know full well the difference between a shuttle and a picker stick. I graduated from Crescent High School in May 1966. By June of that same year, I was sliding down the fire pole at headquarters station of the Greenville City Fire Department as a new hire rookie fireman.

This was my first full time job. I was now a man in uniform, and I really love that job. One day I was hanging outside the second story of the fire station washing windows, when my shift captain came to me holding two letters in his hand addressed to me. He said, "Mac one of these letters you will like because it has lipstick on it, but I'm not so sure about the other letter - you might want to come inside before you open it."

One letter was from my girlfriend, Brenda, and the other was from President Johnson stating "greetings." I entered the United States Army at Fort Jackson, South Carolina on October 13, 1966. I took basic training at Fort Gordon, Georgia and advanced individual training back at Fort Jackson. March 24, 1967, I landed in country at Bien Hoa, Vietnam, Republic of, and was transported to the 90th Replacement Center at Long Binh for in country processing.

After a few days there, I was transported by truck to Cu Chi, home base of the 25th Infantry Division "Tropic

Lightning" to await assignment as an 11 Bravo Infantry soldier. A staff Sergeant said that he wanted the first seven men off this truck to follow him. I was one of the lucky seven. He told us that we now belong to the 1st Brigade, 4th Battalion (Mechanized)23rd Infantry Regiment 25th Infantry Division - track mounted mortar platoon. He said that we would not have to walk the boonies like other "leg" units, but ride on assigned M113 - Armored Personnel Carrier (APC) tracks.

I was overjoyed about this until while out in the jungle, I saw my first M113 track and some of its crew after it was hit by (RPG-7) Rocket propelled grenade. These men were the first of many killed or wounded in action (KIAs and WIAs) that I would see during my tour in Vietnam.

My combat area of operations (AOs) were for the most part, located in Iron Triangle, the Hobo and Boi Loi Woods, Michelin and Filhole Rubber Plantations, Trung Lop, and Trang Bang. Appreciated in numerous combat search and destroy missions, road security for the big Rome plows of the combat engineers during the huge land clearing operations, being reactionary force for other leg units engaged in firefights in the area and engaging in a good number of fights with the Vietcong operating in the area. Many of these fights were with the local force VC.

I participated in five major combat operations consisting of: Manhattan, Barking Sands, Atlanta, Saratoga, and the 1968 TET offensive. On the first four major operations, we mainly tangled with elements of the 9th Main Force Vietcong Division, and the local Cu Chi Battalion. During the TET offensive we fought against elements in the

9th Main Force Vietcong Division, D-14 Vietcong Battalion, and the 88th North Vietnamese Regiment. February 2, 1968, I nearly bought the farm while in the fifty caliber machine gun Turret during an attack by the VC, when a "Charlie" in a spider hole popped up with RPG-7 and let a round fly at my track missing me by inches.

I lived, but he did not. We were engaged in battle in Trang Bang at this time while reinforcing the 3rd Battalion, 22nd Infantry pushing the VC and the NVA out of the area of AP Cho. I later learned that we were engaged in battle with elements of the 271st NVA Regiment, and we were credited with killing 175 of the enemy.

There were three events that put a smile on my face while in this hellhole tour of duty in Vietnam for me. My first event was meeting the movie actor, Charleston Heston, who came to the field to visit the troops while we were on a brief stand down after a tough mission. The old man had sent out hot chow to us and I was standing in line to get some of it when Mr. Heston came down the chow line shaking hands with the troops. We were a filthy, stinking lot that had not shaved or bathed in a number of days. Even the mosquitoes did not want to be around us, but that did not bother Mr. Heston. When he got to me, he shook my hand, wished me well, and admired the pump "trench" shotgun I wore at sling arms.

The second event was getting to come out of the field to see the Bob Hope Christmas show at Cu Chi base camp. To this day, I cannot sing the Christmas song "Silent Night" because it was sung by us on the hill with such heartfelt, lonesome emotion like I have never heard anywhere else. The sad part about it was at the end of the show, Bob Hope said, "Hurry home, you guys," and the reality was that some of those guys standing on that hill would not make it home. That is the bitter part of war.

The third event was getting to go to Australia for six days of rest and relaxation (R&R). After enjoying R&R, I was back in the Nam with my unit and was on a joint mission with the 1st Infantry Division near Lai Khe. Everything was going well until our track shut down on us in a long convoy to Lai Khe. Our squad Sergeant called ahead to our platoon leader and reported our breakdown. The platoon leader, who was a second lieutenant, told us to form a perimeter around our track and wait for the drag party to pick us up with a tank retriever. The only problem with that was he forgot to tell us what company was pulling drag, and he failed to notify the drag unit of our need for a tank retriever.

We sat there on the trail for several hours waiting for the drag party to come and hook us up. I learned later that the drag party never knew of our dilemma and passed us by thinking that we were pulling security for them on the trail. Nightfall came in "Charlie" country, and we were getting a bit nervous being left behind to fend for ourselves. There was a small hamlet just ahead of us, and some of the men folk were standing in the roadway watching. My good buddy, Bod Willett, was a self-made shade tree mechanic. He took a whack at trying to fix the engine while we provided security on the trail. After a while, Bob got the track started up, and we took off like a bat out of hell, scattering Vietnamese left and right standing in the way as we flew by.

It took us nearly an hour to catch up with the drag unit and report our situation. We told the platoon Sergeant of the drag unit that our engine was still acting up, and we needed a tow. A tank retriever pulled up and towed us all the way to Lai Khe. I could have shot our Lieutenant for his foul up that could have gotten us killed or captured.

The 1968 Tet offensive began for us on January 30th with rocket and mortar attacks while in the Hobo Woods, as I was on the fourth watch at my field of fire position at the perimeter. January 31st we were told to saddle up, and we headed for Trang Bang in order to keep Highway 1 clear and to be a blocking force in case the enemy tried to escape to Cambodia. During one firefight with thirty-five VC /NVA killed, and my platoon sergeant must have known that one day in the future I would become a part-time undertaker, so he put me on burial detail as a Rome plow dug a huge trench for a mass grave.

While at Trang Bang, my D.E.R.O.S. came through, and I was told to grab my gear and catch the next chopper outbound for Cu Chi base camp to clear. Two days later, I was on board a freedom bird heading back to the world, the USA. I was now a coming home soldier. Only problem I have about my tour of duty in Vietnam is that no one, other than my combat buddies give a damn for what we went through. I just wish our country could have loved us as much as we loved it and gave our best for it. But that is another story for another day.

After returning home from Nam, I married my teenage sweetheart Brenda on March 31, 1968. When my military time was completed, I later joined the Anderson City Police Department in 1970. I retired as Captain over the Uniform Patrol Division in 1997. I joined the United States Marshall's Service in 1998 as a Special Deputy Court Security Officer and retired in 2015.

Now, I work as a part-time funeral assistant (undertaker) for a local funeral home. My civic organizations include past commander of Post 44 of the American Legion, a life member of the Veterans of Foreign Wars, Post 6087, and a life member of Anderson Disabled Americans. My wife Brenda and I have two children, four grandchildren and three great grandchildren.

In the army I was promoted to the rank of SP/4 E-4 and awarded the National Defense Service Medal, Vietnamese Campaign Medal, Vietnamese Service Cross, Good Conduct Medal, Army Commendation Medal, Combat Infantryman's Badge, Two Overseas Service Bars, Second Class M60 Machine Gun Bar, M16 Expert Badge, Rifle Badge, M14 Rifle Sharpshooter Badge…

I did not particularly like having to go to Vietnam and fight, but I do not regret having been there. If called upon again to serve, I would do so willingly. I was introduced to Vets Helping Vets Anderson by my bestest, best friend Jimmy Burdette back in 2017. The members at Vets Helping Vets Anderson is my medicine for what ails me. I love the camaraderie with fellow veterans.

In Memory of
Lawrence Franklin Merrell
(02/ 23/1918-10/19/2010)
Pearl

"Hey, Dad how are you?" He'd reply, "Is this Tim?" "Yes, Sir, it is" would be my loudest response. Well, this was a special day to call, and I had something on my mind. I queried, "Dad, Where were you on December 7, 1941?" "Huh?" Well, finally he understood I wanted to talk or at least listen, to the tale of where he was when the Japanese attacked. This time I was on my way home, the best time for me to find Dad in the recliner, in from the garden and watching, as best as he could, Jeopardy or Wheel. He proceeded to talk. I pulled off the road and wrote as much as I could on the only available writing material, the front page of The Greenville News. Well, Brothers, Sons, Daughter, Nieces, Nephews, In-laws, and anyone else who may read these words, here goes.

"Boot leave; home in Tigerville," was the short answer. Dad was scheduled for a machinist school, but the Navy inquired whether or not he'd consider Diesel School instead. Boot leave for Frank was cut short just like all the others on leave. New orders were cut sending a young South Carolina boy to the big city, "the coldest place in the world." It was cold, but the people were really nice to Dad. "Like to froze," he recalled. He was housed on the Navy pier, a long pier extending into Lake Michigan with a barracks right there. A trolley track ran between the buildings in a half mile circle. It was a huge structure with tin walls and roof with no insulation, so living there in the winter was a challenge. Frost accumulated on the inside of the roof, melted and rained down on the sailors below. It was an extra blanket for the old southern boy. "They started the USO right there in Chicago." When given liberty, that's sort of free time off for you nonmilitary folks, Frank and buddies went to the USO, got fed sandwiches, and were given tickets, free ones, to movies and ball games. Can you believe he even saw games in the hallowed "Wrigley Field," one of the cathedrals of baseball. The vines were there in 1942. An Italian boy took Dad to a restaurant where he indulged for the first time in a meal of Spaghetti and Meatballs, meatballs the size of baseballs, not like Grandma's country cooking, but good and only thirty-five cents for a big plate and drink.

From Chicago, it was off to Boston and another cathedral, Fenway Park. He had leave coming and the train from Boston to Greenville, South Carolina was one hundred dollars plus seventy-five cents for a meal. So, he and another sailor hitched a ride out to US-1, the highway running North to South along the coast. It took about twenty rides to reach Providence, Rhodes Island and on to New York City. One pack of peanut butter crackers, he liked them way back when, wasn't much to keep a young man going. A cop at Five Points signal dad to come over. Not a good thing as uniformed soldiers and sailors were not supposed to hitchhike. Scared, he approached the policeman." Where are you going, Sailor?" Well, we know where he was going. The cops stopped a car and instructed the driver to take this sailor to the cop at the other end of the Holland Tunnel and then tell that cop to get

186

him a good long ride South. That ride was in a new Buick and headed our direction. When he could stand it no longer, he told the driver, "If you'll stop at a restaurant, I'll buy us some dinner. I'm not broke, I can pay. I've only had crackers since breakfast." For you Merrell's, who like me, eat by the clock; I'm pretty sure the front of his stomach must have been touching his backbone. He really needed to eat. Well, that kind gentlemen pulled into the Howard Johnson restaurant, where Frank had a big dinner with apple pie and ice cream for dessert. The driver wouldn't let him pay a dime. That ride ended in Philadelphia. He caught a trolley, where a homosexual tried to pick him up. Even a country boy could tell something wasn't right about that ride. He followed Dad a couple of blocks, ending that episode something like this, "I'll bust you in the nose." End of story. It was DC to Richmond and on to home. He had four days and hitchhiked back to New York. This time it was duty on a minesweeper. I'm not certain how long, but at least long enough to go to the Yankee Stadium.

Dad came down with a bad sore throat, went to the Infirmary, and was diagnosed by an old Lieutenant Commander, who sent him to the barracks weird directions to gargle warm salt water. That will cure most anything, I thought. In the night frank awoke coughing up blood and lots of it. Gargle, gargle and back to the Infirmary in the morning. This time, however, the younger doctor queried, "Sailor, why haven't you been here already?" Dad explained, "I was here yesterday, and the Lieutenant Commander over there told me to gargle." "I'm going to do something for you. Take this medicine, and…" Well, the something was a trip to the hospital ship to have ruptured tonsils surgically removed. The surgeon and pharmacist mate were working on Dad. The surgeon admonished, "Whatever you do, don't cough!" Cough or choke, Dad chose cough and when he opened his eyes, bother the doctor and the pharmacist mate where covered in blood. Neither was happy, but what's a sailor to do? "I'm going to give you ten days leave to recuperate. Where are you from?" Upon learning the answer, he extended the sick leave to fourteen days and Dad was on the way with extra travel time. This time he sprang for the train.

His tale is this time in a sickly weakened state, the beautiful Thelma talked him into marrying her. At least that's Dad's story. Mother never told such nonsense. Thel didn't know he had saved eight hundred and eighty-five dollars when she married him. No one paid attention to the date, October 31, 1942. If they had, who know what costume ideas would have surfaced. The first month of marriage was spent in the Warwick Hotel in South Portland, Maine, then on to a boarding house. About this time the gleam in Frank's eye materialized in a pregnant bride, a trip to Boston, and a long train ride South for the bride and their first child in the oven.

Well readers, this tale is over. It may be sketchy in parts, it may have been slightly embellished by the teller (Dad) and the scrivener (me), but it should be remembered, this special day, December 7, 2010, the first Pearl without Dad! Thanks Dad, for all the memories.

Your Loving Son,
Tim Merrell

Jon Mooar

My name is Jon Ross Mooar, and I was born in Columbus, Ohio. Then my family moved to Marion, Ohio. Way back when I was in high school, some called me Alfalfa, like the boy in Little Rascals. A few strands of my hair stood straight up on the top of my head. I have an older sister who enjoyed picking on me and a middle sister I called a Prima Donna. My twin sister and I were the youngest of the family, although I am about five minutes older than her. Patti and I were born in October 1942. Our father was killed in an accident when we were about two and a half years old. My mother remarried to a guy in the U.S. Army when we were seven.

We moved to Fort Benning, Georgia and became Army brats. I graduated from Jordan Vocational High School in Columbus, Georgia, in 1961 and joined the Army to get away from my stepdad. I wanted to join the Marine Corps, but there were no Marine Recruiters at Fort Benning. They sent me to Atlanta, Georgia, for my physical. As a kid right out of high school, I did not realize I could have gone to a recruiter there. Returning to Fort Benning, they gave us a nice haircut and issued our supplies. The Sergeant walks in, points at, and numbers the first six guys. He gives us orders to go to Fort Riley, Kansas. Hours later, we were on our way. The Army flew the rest of the guys that were in that building at the time to North Carolina in a DC3. When the plane went down on the way there, the men were killed in the crash. This was my first close call with death that leaves me wondering why I was

189

part of the first six chosen. My mother sent me the article about the plane that went down, headed to Fayetteville, North Carolina.

I enjoyed every minute of basic, especially the shooting of military arms. When we were on the bazooka range, we only got two shots. The guy in front of me missed his mark and I ask him where he was aiming. Thought about it and hit both my shots on the mark. They told me to keep shooting until I missed. After ten or eleven times, I was told to stop shooting because they did not have enough ammunition. Because I learned where to aim, no matter the distance, I could figure out what to do to hit my mark. This made me the only one in the Battalion to receive expert in bazooka.

I tore my Achilles tendon by jumping into a foxhole with a machine gun during training and my leg was put in a cast. The Army had to find me something to do. Given a choice of the Supply or the Arms Room. I chose the Arms Room. Putting me in there with the rifles and everything that goes with them was like putting me in a candy store. For the first time in like ten years, we had an IG inspection. Ours battalion got a hundred percent because of the way I set the Arms Room up.

They changed my MOS to Armor because of my organizational skills. A month later, I received orders to go to Berlin, Germany, because they needed an Armor. I was sick eight of the fourteen days it took to get there on the flat bottom USS Buckner. Days of saltine crackers and seasickness made me glad I did not choose the Navy. I did not know what the ocean was in Columbus, Georgia, located way inland. We landed in Bremerhaven, a seaport in Germany.

This was April 1962. There was a little time before we were to catch the train to Berlin. The three of us ordered a German beer. Sold in nothing less than a liter. Oh, it went down like silk but was twenty-six proof. The two other guys and I did not remember the trip, and we had to go through checkpoints going through East Germany. I ended up profiling the next day with a hangover, learning that was something you had to adjust to. There were all kinds of things happening during that time. While I was in Berlin, America faced dire situations; President Kennedy was assassinated, the Cuba Crisis, the Vietnam War, and we came within one-half hour of another war.

They never got their Armor because I tried out for an Advance Marksmanship (AMU), and I took second. I was only there fifteen to twenty days and made the team. We had to shoot every day, sometimes at the privately owned Rose Range or the military range. We shot in European matches against the French and the British, with our team dominating most matches. There were a few Brits that were good. While I was there, the weather pattern normally matched the United States. We shot 22 calibers inside when it was too cold outside.

There were three of us that traveled to a range regularly to get ready for the next shooting season. We had to go through the usual checkpoints. Most of the east Germans working knew us from prior visit. Sergeant Cramine, a Hawaiian, would take a Taunas Ford and we would drive down to Grafenwöhr to test our rifles on a range. It was early '64, the East Germans stopped an American convoy and refused to let them pass. The convoy had been sitting there for about two days. We come driving up and because we had gotten to know some of the security at the checkpoint; they let us pass after the usual checks. We waved at the convoy as we passed. They televised this on national news. My mom remembered this because she thought the little car driving by with the passengers waving was funny. I told her I was the one driving the car through the checkpoint on our way back to Berlin.

Richard Martin and I became super friends. He played the position of guard on the Nebraska Football team. After Richard played a "joke gone bad" by blowing the door off the coach's locker, the college kicked him out and the Army drafted him. While others were out drinking, we would work out. Then we would max our PT test, earning us a three-day pass. We did fun things like play football, run track, and go out on dates with good-looking girls. He married and they stayed there after he got out of service. Richard taught English in Germany.

I met and married my now ex-wife who had the rank of major but did not wear a uniform. She had a master's in art from Florence, Italy and ran the arts and crafts classes in the Enlisted Men's (EM) Club. We traveled, skied the Zugspitze Mountain on the Austria-Germany border, and married before returning to the states when my services ended in 1964. She was from the Newton, Massachusetts. I wanted to attend college so went back to Newton. I have a son, Jon Eric Mooar and a daughter, Christina Mooar.

We eventually helped care for her Italian parents. Her father, Pat Antonellis, was like a father to me because I never really had a father. My stepfather was very abusive. Pat loved me and would let me do tree work for all his buddies because I had no fear of heights. He came over in 1917 and could not speak a word of English. He pledged to become a citizen and joined the U.S. Army. They put him on a boat and shipped him back to fight against the Germans. His uniform is hanging in the City Hall in Newton, Massachusetts.

When I returned to the states, I went straight to work at ARK-LES Switch Company and took college classes. After joining a local gun club, they ask me to coach. I almost hired on with the Police Department but in the meantime, I went to an interview with Polaroid. My military service and my work record helped me to get the job. When I worked for the ARK-LES Switch Company, I never missed a day or was late, so I ended up getting the job. I began by making cardboard boxes, but within weeks I had several promotions to other departments. I worked for Polaroid for thirty years. During this time, they sent me to machinist school. A school that was set up for one year, I finished in eight months. I was trained in thirty different machines. I took classes in algebra and trigonometry at one college and machinist courses at another college a couple of blocks away from each other. Doing this to help me obtain another paygrade.

When I retired from Polaroid, I moved to New Hampshire. While in New Hampshire, I went to a machine gun shoot and met Sergeant Carlos Hathcock. We sat and talked about coaching techniques for over an hour.

Through my career, I went to seminars on plastics, mold making, schools of computer technology, Computer Aided Design (CAD), etc. I do not waste money because I took bookkeeping and accounting courses at Bentley, one of the biggest accounting colleges. One of the most interesting thing I worked on during my career was a drill with a long bit that had to run quiet while boring through the thick concrete walls. This was to be used to insert a listening device. Through several steps, I completed the task.

We paid bills from my paycheck. I bought anything I purchased for the family from my other jobs, such as grass cutting, tree work, working in a supermarket or a wholesale place. All the while, working a full-time job, coaching and/or taking part in shooting competitions, and remodeling my home. I studied whatever skill I wanted to become proficient in. It was a pleasure to mentor the youth. While I was teaching an advanced junior, Tom Perry put together a Reading Gun Club in Massachusetts for the youth preparing to go to college. After practicing during the day, we would relax and have a question-and-answer session at night. I shared the importance of writing shooting diaries, the course I taught at MIT.

These diaries prove important in just about any skill you want to succeed in. They were to write about their range, what worked, and what did not work. Include the reasons, if known. I coached at MIT in Boston, the biggest engineering school in the nation, from 1973 until 1982. Two kids who had never shot before, then turned out for Olympic trials. My practice secessions were touch and expected. I told them I worked a job at Polaroid, coached at MIT, and shooting for two different gun clubs. To succeed, they need to prove their dedication. I was proud of my kids, I instructed, and they respected me. They were very intelligent students because MIT was a highly academic school. They became distinguished individuals.

These students kept me young. At thirty-five, I drove a souped-up Dodge Charger with a 400 cubic inches engine set up really high in the back. I attended classes to keep one step ahead of my students. One of my heroes, Sergeant Pulliam, who wrote books on subjects such as a three-position shooting, taught one of my classes. He was part of the AMU unit at Fort Benning, Georgia. He calls me up to the podium in front of three hundred students and asks me to teach about using diaries there.

My mother and stepdad lived next door to a guy named Sergeant Brown in Columbus, Georgia. He and Gary Anderson translated the Russian book, Competitive Shooting. It was about muscle tone and other important aspects of competitive shooting. I had studied his books. In 1977, I got to visit him at his home, and it was like walking into a museum. He had been an Army coach for over twenty years. I gave him Papa's razor and other items from WWI because he collected antiques and took good care of them. To him, it was priceless, and he would send me all kinds of paperwork from famous shooting coaches. I had the honor of being his friend. We had many conversations with him over the phone and in person. He was a very interesting person, and I never tired of his constructive conversations.

I met my wife Dee one weekend after she and her friends bowled as a team in a bowling league. A group of my friends borrowed a military police jeep with a white stripe around it and picked me up. We stopped in the place where Dee and her friends were having a sandwich and drinks. I asked Dee, the most petite lady there, to dance. We have been dancing together for forty-three years. Dee was a hard worker. After quitting high school to support her family, she went back to school at forty-two to earn her GED. She graduated valedictorian and went on to college. Dee graduated with honors with two of her children. Then worked for the Stationery Company and RCA as an engineering aide. We would go to the Horseshoe Lounge, where the band played 50s' music and we enjoyed dancing. It was Sadie Hawkins Day when she asked me if I wanted to marry her. We had a festive event when we married that included music and dancing.

Dee is the sweetest and most compassionate woman I have ever known. She stayed by my side and supported me as I continued to work, coach and travel across the nation doing competitive shooting. Dee spent many days and nights alone. I woke up and realized how hard this must have been on her, when I only had three days and nights alone in an empty house with nothing to do. I had earned twenty-four points out of the thirty required and gave up pursuing the National Distinguished Marksmanship Badge. She questioned me if I felt forced out. I want her to know she is my Distinguished Award; far above any award I could ever receive.

My first award was in Columbus, Georgia, when I was in high school. I took 8th in the nation. In 1977, I joined the 169th Infantry Battalion of the Connecticut National Guard. Then in 1980 at Little Rock, Arkansas, I shot a record for clean off-hand that still stands. The Commander that ran the Marksmanship Program (Homer Pearson) for the Army handed me the trophy and said, "Good shooting. Get a haircut!" While coaching at MIT for over eight years, I distinguished in small-bore three-position shooting. I won over five hundred awards throughout my shooting career.

No one should take for granted their fine home, education, and family. There are kids growing up without mothers or fathers because the parents signed the dotted line to serve their country. They gave the ultimate sacrifice, their lives. The military has been good to me, allowing me to pursue my dream of competition shooting. The youth of today have more opportunities and choices. There are many career choices in the military. My advice for the youth would be to study what you want to become. Take the tests the military gives you, pay attention, do what they ask you to do, and be willing to learn new things.

We moved to Anderson, South Carolina, after visiting a friend from a church we attended in New Hampshire who had moved to Pendleton, South Carolina. We were on our way to vacation in Florida. When we returned home, our driveway had three and a half inches of solid ice and the roof had four feet of snow, which I spent three days removing. We remembered the weather and scenery of South Carolina, which reminded us of New Hampshire.

They have replaced both of my knees. After having a pacemaker installed and four stents, I would work out at the gym for a couple of hours and then walk at the mall. That is where Al Lane saw my veteran's hat and invited me to attend a Vets Helping Vets Anderson meeting. I liked to help others by cutting grass, trimming, and building ramps for those who need it. I can help more veterans through our programs.

Often, I would read the death notices in the paper and try to attend a veteran's funeral when I noticed there was no family to honor him and pay my last respect. Now, I am a First Lieutenant in the Honor Guard. My job is to get everything ready for the firearms and flags; repairing when needed. It is an honor to take care of the veteran's family and help give them closure.

My advice: If you want to get ahead in life, educate yourself and practice, practice, practice!

Jessie A. Moore

This story is being told by his wife, Maryanne Moore, on behalf of Jessie Moore.

Jessie enlisted in the USMC Marine Corps in Dallas, Texas (1988-1991). Several of his uncles served in the Army and Marine Corps. He had always planned to serve his country.

He completed basic training at Camp Pendleton, California. He was a Corporal (E4) as a MSSG-24 Motor Transport Dispatcher with the 8th Battalion. Served as a Motor Vehicle Operator for eight months and a Logistic Vehicle System Operator for two years. He was stationed at Camp Lejeune, North Carolina. Jessie was awarded Rifle Expert, National Defense Service Medal, Good Conduct Medal, Sea Service Deployment Medal, and received a Letter of Appreciation from the commandant. His military education included Motor Vehicle Operator, Logistics Vehicle System Operator, and Nutrition course.

In 1989-1990 he had the opportunity to serve on the amphibious cargo ship, USS EL PASO (LKA-117) visiting ports in Spain, Italy, France, Israel, Tunisia, and Puerto Rico. Jessie said that he enjoyed this cruise because this was his first time out of Texas and the USA. This journey was an eye-opening experience for Jessie as it exposed him to culture, food and people outside the United States. By this opportunity of travel, it awakened him to seek more than just Texas.

Upon returning from the Mediterranean cruise, he broke his foot and ankle during a training exercise. As a result, it left him in a cast for two years, leading to a medical discharge from Camp Lejeune. His platoon preceded to Desert Storm without him.

The ending of his military career led him to work various jobs. He then went to join his family, who had a restaurant, and pursued a career in hospitality and nutrition at Lamar College. After college, he joined a restaurant chain that brought him to South Carolina in the 90s. After several years dedicated to the restaurant business, he could not spend enough time with his two daughters and changed careers. He then went into sales in the automotive industry for several years.

Jessie was very well versed in many skills prior to his service. He learned electrical, welding, car repairs, and A/C repairs. These skills helped him in the Marine Corps and made him a very well-rounded individual. He gained excellent organizational skills, among other skills. Jessie always had a very strong personality, and was determined, loyal, and an great employee with an exceptional work ethic. As a leader, he was always the guy you would want next to you or pushing you to do better. He was well liked by all his peers, friends, and colleagues. With a great sense of humor, he has also been known to be the prankster when given the opportunity for a good laugh. He is the type of guy that has all the resources and is able to get the job done. Gladly, giving the shirt off of his back to help anyone in need. If Jessie did not know how to fix it, he always knew a guy that could help.

Back in 2001, the only regret Jessie ever spoke of was that he could not go back to the Marines after 9/11. It changed him and his outlook on life and how the world would change. I came to Greenville, South Carolina on September 10, 2001, and also was forever changed by the tragic event that day of 9/11. We met on December 30, 2001, finding each other on Match.com. Our first date was several events and conversations that lasted sixteen hours, and we knew we were destined for each other. We got married eight weeks later.

He had two little girls that were a package deal. It was a blessing that we found each other. Jessie is from Texas, and I am from Florida with family in New York. It was a tough decision where we would get married. My father was watching the travel channel and said, "I'll pay you a thousand dollars to stop talking about this and go to Las Vegas." So, we did! Life was good for several years, working hard, playing hard, family trips, vacations, and building many memories.

With an interest in finance around 2003, Jessie became a licensed mortgage broker and enjoyed helping families obtain financing for their first home or dream homes. By 2007, when the recession came about, he had to change gears again and went back into the car business which brought us to Anderson, South Carolina. In 2016, he had enough time spent burning the pavement and went back into finance doing mortgages and refinancing until 2018.

One of his dreams was to be a mentor to our youth and share his passion for fishing and being on the water. He wanted to have a boat big enough to take out troubled children and show them basic survival skills. Jessie always said that if you teach a child to love the water and they will stay out of trouble. Almost succeeding in his dream until now, when his health issues put an end to that dream. He believed that all should serve in the military as they will come out respectable people in society. They should have integrity, strong values, pride, and be hard working individuals; an asset to anyone they come across to in life. He had a motto on his computer that said, "Get Busy Living or Get Busy Dying."

November 2016, Jessie was not feeling well and misdiagnosed for two years following. He became bed bound before finding out he had a spontaneous spinal fluid leak in his back, which was causing him so much pain, headache and dizziness. After several procedures and misdiagnosis, his health had ups and downs. His final procedure on February 8, 2018, changed our lives and paths forever. During the surgery, he obtained a brain bleed in the thalamus that left him wheelchair bound with many issues. Jessie became unable to work or enjoy the same quality of life he always had. Now he is unable to perform all his abilities to fulfill his dreams on his own.

However, as several doors closed on us, new doors opened. By not having the ability to work anymore and needing a full-time caregiver, I had to step into this role. This allowed us to meet and know a different aspect in life and challenges as they serve us now.

We currently look for any opportunities that Jessie could enjoy with his state of health and limitations. We embraced his military affiliations and joined the Marine

Corps League and Vets Helping Vets Anderson. Our introduction to VHVA was from a mutual friend of ours who was a member of the Quilts of Valor. The friend invited us to a meeting, and he was wrapped that day with his own quilt of valor. It was such an amazing feeling to be surrounded by so many veterans who embraced us like family. We have not missed many meetings in the last three years since joining.

During this time, we have received help, support or guidance from the following organizations: Vets Helping Vets Anderson, Upstate Warrior Solutions, When Life Sucks, Patriot Partners of the Upstate, Purple Heart Homes Golden Corner Chapter, Quilts of Valor Anderson, DAV Anderson, Upstate-Carolina Adaptive Golf, Roger C. Peace (Prisma) Rehab recreational activities, Wild Hearts Equine Therapy Center, Pontoon fishing with Vets Helping Vets Anderson, Wives of Vets Helping Vets, several neighbors and friends.

Thank you to everyone and all these organizations that fill up our calendar with so many events that allow us to continue to enjoy life as we know it now. Having all our veterans and new friends keep us motivated and active within our community is the biggest blessing and encouragement to survive our daily challenges. This story is dedicated to all of you who support us and make us get up and smile each day.

With the help of the organizations mentioned, Jessie is able to enjoy his hobbies of golf, boating, fishing, archery, grooming horses, and more. We have found ways to travel and enjoy important family time. Jessie misses and thinks of both his beautiful girls each day and wishes he could spend more time with them and his two grandsons. Life moves pretty quickly, and you never know when your day comes that you either cannot live life anymore on this earth or survive what life gives you. Do not waste your days leaving things unsaid or with regrets. Aim to not cause or be the cause of pain to anyone. No one warned us that life can be hard, and it does not come with an instruction manual. Just do not give up and keep at it! Thank you for being part of our story.

Mary Ellen Mullikin

I always try to be the best at everything I do. I was born and raised in Carlsbad, New Mexico, The Land of Enchantment, the fourth of five children. My first year of college was spent as a student in the Philippine Islands as a Rotary Exchange Student. That is when I first got sand in my shoes to travel. Upon my return, I graduated from New Mexico State University, "Go Aggies," with BS in Home Economics Education.

My first job after graduating was teaching in El Paso, Texas at Austin High School, placing students in home economics related jobs. During my second year teaching I told my dad that I wanted to join the Peace Corps. When asked why, I told him that I had witnessed the good things they were doing in the Philippine Islands, and I wanted to travel and be part of that. He had the perfect answer for me, to join the military.

At the time my dad, Stanley W. Johnston, Sr,, was a Brigadier General in the New Mexico Army National Guard. He was a WWII hero, with many decorations for his service and bravery. My oldest brother, Stanley W. Johnston Jr., was a full time Major in the NMARNG. So, in no time I had my right hand raised to join the Women's Army Corps in 1976, and I became a direct commission WAC.

In Fort McClellan, Alabama, I learned all of my basic training skills. I also learned what poison oak and ivy are. Then I returned to NMARNG, as their first female officer that was not a nurse. My first real assignment was in 642nd

Maintenance Company in Las Cruces, New Mexico. I loved that unit. Most of our work was at Dona Ana Range Camp, outside of Fort Bliss, Texas. My Ordnance Training (OD) was at Aberdeen, Maryland, where my team of three female officers beat the guys taking apart and reassembling 1/4T, then a 2 ½T engines.

I met my husband when he was attending a course at Fort Bliss Texas. He was a member of the South Carolina Army National Guard (SCARNG), in the Advanced course. We honeymooned to South Carolina, in 1982, where I transferred to the SCARNG Signal Corps. Assigned to the 228th Signal Brigade, then the 151st Signal Battalion. My Signal Corps training was at Fort Gordon, Georgia.

In 1996, I went full time, Active Guard Reserves (AGR), and the 151st Signal Battalion, in the S3 shop. My proud achievement: I was the first South Carolina Army National Guard female company Commander. My unit was D/151st Signal Battalion. I am still very proud of that, and my unit, because those members are super soldiers.

Once again, I branched transferred to Air Defense Artillery (ADA). I received that training at Fort Bliss, Texas where I graduated with honors, in a man's world I should add. I have served in many positions since then. I have been in the S/G1, S2, S3/G3, and in the G4 shop to serve until my retirement. I have branch transferred from OD, to SIG, to ADA. In my twenty-eight years of service, I did get my traveling in. I've served in many places CONUS (to include Alaska and Hawaii) and OCONUS to include Korea, Japan, Egypt, and Germany.

After 28 years, I was glad to retire and get back into a different war zone, teaching. I was even more glad to retire completely. I met many wonderful and some not so wonderful people while serving. Many life coping skills were learned while serving. I am extremely proud to have served my country. I think every able-bodied person should serve their country. I have been married for forty years and have two wonderful daughters. I have enjoyed the Vets Helping Vets Anderson. I think it is a wonderful organization and have enjoyed meeting other veterans.

Scotty Murdock

My name is Denny Murdock. I am called Scotty because my grandparents on my mother's side migrated from Scotland. My grandfather had a name that was just impossible for Americans to pronounce so they started calling him Scotty. After I was born, he started calling me Scotty. We were known as big Scotty and little Scotty. This has stuck with me all my life, and that has been good.

I grew up in North Central, Minnesota on a eighty acre dairy farm. Forty acres were open and tillable while the other forty acres were wooded and flat as a tabletop. I was the youngest of three boys. My parents bought the farm with a four room farmhouse, an unfinished upstairs, a barn for twelve milk cows, a separate one-style garage, and an outhouse. The outhouse was still in use when I left home.

In 1946, I got polio and spent late '46 and most of '47 in the hospital in the Twin Cities. By the time I was eight years old, I was working on the farm with my brothers. Our first major chore was to clear the wooded forty acres. The big timber we hauled to a neighbor who had a sawmill. All the rest went into firewood for the house. In those days everything was hand work, so we grew up quick and tough. My dad worked away from home in the iron mines until around 1953. Every time he got extra money; he bought the adjoining property which was mostly wooded. He again cut the trees for logs and the rest for firewood. With the help from a few cases of dynamite and a stump puller we ended up with two hundred forty acres of good farmland.

My parents were very loving and also very strict. We learned respect, honesty, and hard work. I would not want it any other way. I attended school through grades one through twelve in a class of thirty. A recruiter visited our school. I knew I would be up for draft. I enlisted in the Army during my senior year and two days after graduation I was in Fort Leonard Wood, Missouri for basic training. Basic was no problem for me except learning the army way; The hurry up and wait. My oldest brother was a first lieutenant in Alaska at that time and he had told me a lot of what to expect.

Then on to Camp Poke, Louisiana for Advance Infantry Training. When I enlisted, the recruiter asked me what field I wanted to get into. I told him that I would like to be in the engineers, and he promised me that was all set up. Found out I was in the heavy weaponry infantry not the engineers. I was getting about sixty-two dollars a month plus room and board when I was offered a chance to go to jump school and get another fifty-five dollars a month.

I grabbed that and went to Fort Benning, Georgia. When I completed jump school, I was offered a chance to go to Parachute Rigger school at Fort Lee, Virginia. We had a great commander there. He was a senior jumper at that time and wanted his Master wings. Somehow he had connections with the local Army and Air Force bases and got planes in every weekend to get in the jumps needed. He selected eight of us to build our jumps, also. We would go down to the pack shed every evening and pack up a bunch of shoots for the next weekend. Sometimes we had C-123s but mostly it was Army Otters, Caribous, CH-34 and C-119. We would strap on a chute and up we would go, jump, hit the ground, strap on another chute and repeat for the full weekend. Sometimes making ten and twelve jumps a day for Saturday and Sunday. By the end of Rigor school, I was getting rather gung ho, so I signed up for Ranger and Special Forces school and headed off to Fort Bragg, North Carolina. Now that was an eye opener, but being a hard wrapped farm kid, I got through there without a hitch. There was no horseplay there it was all business. It was hard but I am glad I went through it. Upon completion, I was sent to Fort Dix, New Jersey for my first ocean tour on the USS Simon B Buckner for a nine-day sea cruise to Bremerhaven, Germany. Then on the 10th Special Forces Group at Bad Tolz, Germany.

That part of Germany was beautiful, and I loved it. However, it was just eighteen years after the war, and you could still see a lot of the damage. I knew it was a lot better than Vietnam

I did not get sent on any deployments like a lot of the veterans in our group although I served from 1960-1965 during the Vietnam era. While stationed in Germany, we were sent on three missions, two were covert: one to South America and one to West Africa. Those were strictly supply and education training. What we were supplying to both locations were 106mm Recoilless Rifles, about a dozen water-cooled 30 caliber machine guns, 250 caliber machine guns, ammunition and the Browning Automatic Rifles (BARs). The Army was phasing out the BARs and coming out with the M-60 machine gun. We were dropped with a huge supply, around one hundred BARs, and the other equipment in both places.

When we met with the forces, they were guerilla forces and we had to train them to operate them.

If anyone ever wants to know how to mount a 106mm on a beat up Datsun pickup, just ask me. First you have to turn it into a convertible, so the barrel points forward. In the jungle there were no cutting torches or metal saws, so like all good soldiers we improvise. We beat out the windshield and rear window, rolled down the side windows and wrapped DET cord around the four corner supports and fired it off, instant convertible.

In 1964, allies were being kicked out of Europe. Jordan was setting up Airborne Forces at that time. They were an ally and had sent a number of individuals (I think there were fourteen altogether) up to a place called St. Andre, France, basically the aerial supply unit for the entire European theatre. These individuals were to be taught how to pack cargo on the platform, rig the 100-foot diameter cargo shoots, and extraction shoots so they could do air drops. I think we were there about five weeks if I remember right, otherwise, I was just a regular soldier around in Germany.

While in Germany, I and others made hundreds of jumps trying to figure out a way to make the high altitude low opening (HALO) idea work. It would only work if you were inserting a single jumper at any time, because of the noise of the canopy popping open. It is like when you are hunting and you hear one shot, you cannot tell just where it came from, but if you hear a half a dozen you can pinpoint the location. Eventually the army came out with the new airfoil type shoots and changed to the high altitude high opening (HAHO) that was well after my time.

I really enjoyed my time in Europe. When off duty or on leave, I would jump on my motorcycle and go. Free Europe was not that big in the sixties so you could hit two or three countries in a weekend.

My tour was up in May of 1965, and I got called in for a re up talk. France was vacant and Germany was full. They were going to offer me one stripe, a two hundred and fifty dollars reenlistment bonus, and a transfer. When I asked where, they said probably to the 5th or the 7th SF Group for they needed men badly. I asked, "Didn't the 5th and the 7th just get sent to Nam?" The answer was yes. That was when I said that if that war were being run by the military I would go in a minute, but not when it's being run by a bunch of idiots in D.C. that are not even qualified to be Boy Scouts. So, a few weeks later I was loading up for my second sea cruise, believe it or not on the USS Simon Buckner, back to the good old USA.

I was awarded the Overseas Service Ribbon, Good Conduct Medal, Sharp-shooters Badge, Infantry Badge, and others. The one I treasure the most is my Master Jump wings.

In April of 1965 I got out and headed back to northern Minnesota. I got married, had three children and worked in residential building construction until 1969. Then I was offered a job in law enforcement. I still worked in construction on the side.

In 1975, I started a maple syrup company called Gun Lake Sugarbush. I had a neighbor with forty acres of big hard

Maple trees. I made a deal to tap them and give him a case of syrup each year. We would put out around 2500 taps and produced 300 to 400 gallons a year depending on the climate.

After five years, I sold that and started teaching motorcycle safety classes for the Motorcycle Safety Foundation. Then in 1984, I started a fiberglass manufacturing company called North Star Manufacturing, LLC and built cargo trailers for the big touring motorcycles. Then I sold that business in 1990. All the while I was still working in law enforcement. I retired from the law enforcement in 1991 and moved to Grand Junction, Colorado.

In 1992, I got with the Department of Highway Safety, and I started the Western Colorado Motorcycle Safety Program (WCMSP). I taught the entire west slope, which is everything west of the mountains from Wyoming to New Mexico, until 2002 when I retired again.

I met my wife, Pamela, in Grand Junction while teaching the motorcycle safety class. We got married in a hot air balloon. She surprised me with a ride in a hot air balloon for my birthday. This had been part of my bucket list. We have been married over twenty-two years.

Her parents had moved to Hilton Head, South Carolina, and we went to visit them for their 50th Anniversary. We came through Anderson visiting the surrounding mountains and Hartwell Lake. Pam, an avid golfer, inquired about the reasonably priced golf courses.

Vets Helping Vets Anderson is the first veteran's group I belong to that actually does something for veterans. I am so proud of our veterans and enjoy meeting with them every

213

Wednesday. It is an honor for me to help take care of lawn duties at Dolly Cooper Veterans Cemetery.

Lois Nash
In Memory of
(1921- 2011)
Born to Fly

In the M.J. Dolly Cooper Veteran's Cemetery in Anderson, South Carolina is the headstone of the greatest patriot I have personally ever known.

While attending Michigan State Teachers College, Louis Louise Lancaster Nash completed the Civilian Pilot Training Program established by President Franklin Delano Roosevelt. She had dreamed of becoming a pilot since her first plane ride at the age of five in Dearborn, Michigan. "As soon as we were high enough to see all the way into Canada, I knew I wanted to fly a plane -- not just riding one!"

In 1943 Lois graduated college and joined other women pilots and headed to Sweetwater, Texas, after being accepted into the Army Air Force's experimental flight training program for women. In this program, women pilots trained men to fly planes for the WWII war effort. As part of their training, the women pilots often flew as high as 20,000 feet, towing targets for the B-24 gunners to shoot.

Lois and ninety-four other young women pilots paid their own way to get to Sweetwater and become WASP Class 8. Less than half of them earned their WASP wings. In all, 1,102 women completed the ten WASP classes. Of those, Thirty-eight WASP's ultimately lost their lives in service to our country.

Lois never missed an opportunity to fly. She trained WWII pilots to fly planes, she trained me in on the equipment itself, she transported wounded soldiers, and she also delivered planes from their manufacturers to strategic military bases. Her favorite plane was the B-26 bomber because it was, in her words, "the fastest and most maneuverable." In all, Lois learned, taught, mastered, and flew sixteen different kinds of aircraft during her eighteen months of military service.

Meanwhile, her husband, Albert E Nash was serving in Italy and North Africa. After the WASP program was disbanded in 1944, she and Albert soon returned home where they started a family and raised two sons. Lois continued to fly now and then just for the thrill of flying and also to keep her flying license current. In 1977 President Jimmy Carter signed legislation that militarized the WASP, making them all officers, retroactive to 1943. When Albert Nash retired he and Lieutenant Lois Nash moved to Lake Keowee in South Carolina. She became an active church member in nearby Seneca. And that is where we met, in church, after my family moved to Anderson County in 2002. Lois was as active in church as she had been with her flying passions. She served on the church board, planned our hymns and services, and lead our Wednesday evening testimony services.

Lois frequently spoke to upstate men's and women's organizations about her WWII and WASP experiences. And not a Veteran's Day or Memorial Day passed in which she wasn't a parade's Grand Marshall, a keynote speaker, or a Guest of Honor somewhere in our country. She loved nothing more than arriving in the pilot or co-pilot seat of a plane. When she put on her Dress Blues, she radiated patriotism and pride as much as anyone who ever wore the uniform. She savored every salute she ever received. Lieutenant Nash was passionate about the greatness of this country, one that had given her the opportunity to learn, to travel, and to fulfill her dreams alongside men with similar dreams. She never spoke of one gender, race, or class as being superior to another. She talked, instead, about how we all have God-given strengths and abilities and that the freedom and opportunity to use those strengths and abilities for good are worth fighting for.

Last time I was with Lois she treated everyone to lunch after church services. She then invited us to her home on lake Keowee to see the Congressional Medal of Honor presented to her a few weeks earlier by President Obama in Washington D.C. She and one hundred seventy-four other WASP's attended that special ceremony. Each WASP received one of the medals, the highest honor that Congress can award a civilian. It remains the largest event ever held in our nation's Capital building.

At the end of our visit to her home. Lois gifted me several of her religious reference books. Some are very old and rare. I keep them near the folded American flag from atop the casket of another of my favorite WWII heroes, Dad.

Lieutenant Lois Nash was given a full military funeral in M.J. Dolly Cooper Veteran's Cemetery on Easter Sunday morning April 24, 2011, twelve days after her ninetieth birthday. She took her final flight, yes, still carrying an active flying license. **Written by: Jay Wright, Foothills Writers Guild Historian.**

Joe Purdy

My name is Joseph Joe Purdy. I was born November 1953 in Savannah, Georgia, the second of six children. My dad's career involved designing paper mills, so we moved a lot. We lived in most of the southern states from Savannah to Jessup, Georgia to Orlando, Florida to Cleveland, Tennessee to Laurel, Mississippi and finally settling in Birmingham, Alabama.

I finished school at Banks High School. After high school, I received my invite from Uncle Sam to sunny Vietnam. Not wanting to be a foot soldier or jarhead. The word jarheads was used by sailors back during WWII because when the Marines wore their dress blue uniform, the high collar made them look like their heads were popping out of a Mason Jar. I planned on going into the Navy. My mother suggested I talk to a man about the Coast Guard. I had no clue who they were. After learning they were a peacetime service who saved lives I signed up.

My Coast Guard service began at Alameda, California for boot camp. My first duty station was an 82-foot Point Steel (WPB-82359) cutter out of Oswego, New York where I met my wife, Bonnie. We patrolled the big sailboat races, did public relations work, and performed search and rescue work.

One great experience was going through the Weiland Canal. The canal is located between Lake Erie and Lake Ontario. While in New York, I earned the nickname "Grits" due to the habit of going to breakfast and asking for grits and red eyed gravy.

Early 1974 while in New York, I swapped stations with a guy out of Miami, Florida. I got the rank of third class before leaving New York. The day I left New York, we had six feet of snow on the ground. I was so grateful to leave New York for sunny Florida. Upon arriving in Florida, I was assigned to the small boat docks. I soon learned this was the busiest Coast Guard station in the world.

Within a few months, I became a Federal Boarding Officer and a Coxswain. We operated two boat crews per day and occasionally we needed three crews. Our first boat crew operated on the average of eighteen to eighteen and a half hours a day. The second boat crew averaged sixteen to seventeen hours per day. My longest day was thirty-four hours rescuing boaters.

While in Miami I had the pleasure along with John Meddor to train Customs how to operate their boat, learn the area, and assist in rescue work if they were close to a boat in trouble.

I never saw combat. My combat was with Mother Nature and people in trouble. I dealt with both Cuban and Haitian refugees. I had a few guns shoved in my face by Spanish people who claimed they did not speak English. I was really surprised how quickly they learned English when they were told they were going to jail.

One of the fun things we did was to send new recruits to all the six boats stationed there to look for relative bearing grease. After visiting the ships, one came back with a small box with a nut inside. She was mad at me, and I was the target when she threw it. We laughed about it and got along with each other. That was a good thing as she was assigned to my crew that month.

I was brought up on charges for having beer on my boat. At the captain's mast there was no one to accuse me nor no one to witness whether they saw a beer on my boat. So as the military usually does, I was found guilty and lost my 2nd Class stripe. This ended my desire to make the military my career.

After getting out of the service, we moved to Athens, Georgia Where I did commercial construction. About a year later we moved to Belton, South Carolina to start a business with a former roommate and crew member. That fell through when his wife and kids moved back to Miami. It forced him to go back also.

I went back into commercial construction. A year later I went to work for Wayne's Overhead Doors. I worked there for thirteen years on two different occasions. I went to Tri-County Tech under the GI Bill and took welding, auto body repair, and machine shop CNC programming. I worked at several shops doing fabrication, running lathes, grinders, and mills. I also did welding and silver soldered carbide into tools. I also did whole house water filtration system installations.

I worked for the last fourteen years at Rexroth, a Bosch Company using my machinist and welding skills. On February 28th, 2021, I retired. My wife and I have been married for 49 years on August 17, 2023. We have two children and four grandchildren. My daughter April married Lyle Dempsey and they have one son Kaden. They live in Spartanburg. My son Travis married Jorden Vaughn and they have three children: Payton, Haley, and Bentley. They live a few miles down the road from us.

I am enjoying my retirement for I have always enjoyed hunting, camping and all outdoor activities. My hobbies include guns and reloading, also flyfishing and tying flies.

The military taught me responsibility how to overcome my fears, how to make split second decisions, and forced me to grow up. I was put in a position where I had to make life saving decisions. I was responsible for my crew's life as well as these being rescued. I was also responsible for both boats. On slow days we sometimes created our own calls and went fishing. Sometimes we would go free diving for lobster.

I am truly honored to be part of Vets Helping Vets Anderson and I am glad to be amongst my fellow veterans and heroes. As I told my family, I have finally found my niche in life - helping people.

Alan Ramsey

My name is Otis Alan Ramsey, or "Ram," a nickname I picked up in the military. I enlisted in the National Guard in September 1978, and later transferred to an active AGR position. Ann, my wife of forty-seven years, stayed at home, raised three children, and held down the home front while I devoted thirty-one years to military service. We are from Anderson, South Carolina. I joined the military to make a career and to support my family. My father, Otis Ramsey, had served in World War II, and my brother Frankie Ramsey, served in the Vietnam War. It was in my blood to follow in their footsteps.

Adapting to military life was normal. I served in a time of respect and discipline. Basic training was non-stop, with rigorous training and little sleep. It was a mind game, just getting through one day at a time, not worrying about the next day. Drill Sergeants had no mercy and enjoyed the continuous tormenting of their recruits. I survived Boot Camp and watched as the next group of recruits took our place, and the Drill Sergeants did it all over again.

I served in different units stateside, Iraq, Kuwait, and Afghanistan during my service. My career included Communications, Electrical and Electronics, Missile Systems, Air Defense, Field Artillery, Support Battalion, Transportation, and Logistics. A highlight was sharing a summer camp in Egypt with my son, who is also in the military.

Deployments were long and stressful for soldiers, and the families left at home. Awards and medals were presented for soldiers' service to be displayed on uniforms. But the medal can't tell the whole story. War changes a person's outlook on life. I don't think a soldier ever entirely comes home after the war. A small piece is left behind on each battlefield.

Serving with my units was a life-changing experience. We learned to depend on and trust one another, knowing our life depended on it. To ease tension, someone was always clowning around or pranking someone. But there were serious times, too, prayers and hopes we would see home again.

Coming home and retiring after thirty-one years was one of the hardest things I have done. Adjusting back to civilian life was a challenge. Things in the workforce have drastically changed. Work ethics are nonexistent, and respect for any authority is gone. The world has changed.

Serving in the military helped me get where I am today. I have a blessed life filled with family, friends, and memories. I made life-long friends while serving, and we share a kindred spirit. I loved serving in the military and would do it all over if given the opportunity. I hope and pray that my service paid honor to those who served before me. For the ones who didn't make it back, they are the true HEROES in my book.

SFC Retired Otis Alan Ramsey "Ram"

Don Rioux

My name is Donald Paul Rioux, and I was born June 4, 1941, into a family of five boys. I was born in Syracuse, New York. At the age of four, my family moved to West Hartford, Connecticut.

Brother number one entered the Marines at seventeen, number two joined the Merchant Marines and then the Navy, and number three joined the Army Reserve. I was number four and joined the Air Force and stationed in France. Number five brother joined the Navy and was assigned to the James K Polk Guided Missile Submarine stationed in Roda, Spain.

My father worked as a tool and die maker for Brewer Manufacturing making aircraft parts for Pratt and Whitney manufacturing. My mother also worked for Pratt and Whitney polishing propeller parts for B17 bombers. My formative years were spent going to school and visiting my grandparents on their farm located on the shore of Oneida Lake, New York.

On November 5, 1959, I joined the U.S. Air Force and went to Lackland Air Force Base, San Antonio, Texas and then to Amarillo, Texas for Unit Recorder Administration. From Amarillo, I was sent to Evenrue, France at the 350 Air Division Europe to provide support for C130 aircraft.

I was initially assigned to the aircraft out of service unit to supply needed parts from air material areas in the United States. I had to learn to keypunch IBM cards for parts and transmit them to the United States. This was my initiation into data processing which I worked out after discharge from the Air Force. Our central responsibility was to support the Army and Marine units in Germany and various countries in Eastern Europe, South Africa and the Congo. My duty station was located sixty miles southwest of Paris, France, trips to Paris were often and at times very entertaining. Paris was the headquarters for the Supreme Headquarters Allied Powers Europe (SHAPE) all troops in Europe are controlled by this Headquarters, unless some special unit, i.e., Navy Seals, Green Beret, Rangers, etc. The Army guys would have a pass that had a time limit, whereas the Air Force types were on Class A pass with no restrictions leaving the young ladies ready to play!! And no one but the lonely Air Force dudes to provide the service, all were very willing and able to complete the duty.

My base responsibilities were to be assigned to the second shift duty which started at 4:00 PM and ended at 12:00 AM. Just in time for the opening of chow hall for midnight service, and a very great time to be fed in the military! There were actually times when very tasty steaks were left over from earlier dinners and left for us poor individuals to consume.

One time a B58 was at Paris Air Show and was challenged to outfly a fighter aircraft as they circle the airfield. The B58 easily beat the fighter, unfortunately as it crossed the field it climbed and rolled over causing, what later was described as an aileron freeze, the aircraft to nose down and crash in a farm field adjacent to the airport. All crew members were killed. As extra duty we went to the site and recovered the aircraft and crew.

Other duty that I was fortunate to do was to operate the projectors in the base theater. I had to inspect the film before and repair any breaks or cracks that I found. It was quite interesting switching between projectors for the featured movies. I was discharged on March 20, 1963, at McGuire Air Force Base, New Jersey.

My work in the Air Force operating keypunch and verifying equipment peaked my interest in Data Processing. Because of that, I went to Buffalo Data Processing School in Buffalo New York where I learned how to program IBM sorters, collators, and unit record machines used to produce various reports, including payroll production. Upon graduation from Buffalo Data Processing, I was hired by Lipe-Rollway Corporation operating their unit record equipment on their third shift operation. The next equipment I trained on was the 1440 computer which included disk and tape storage. I left Lipe-Rollway to take a job at Farmers and Traders Life Insurance Company doing their payroll and other reports.

After Farmers, I enrolled in Lemoyne College in Syracuse, New York, graduating in June 1970 with a BS in Industrial Relations with a minor in Economics. After graduation from Lemoyne, I was hired by the City of Syracuse as the Emergency Management supervisor of the State program for hiring and training individuals for jobs with the City and County of Onondaga, New York.

From there I was interviewed and selected by the Rotary Foundation to participate in a program to inform the Indian Rotary about our system of government in the States. The program was sponsored by the foundation for five members from various positions from business, education, and private ownership. We stayed with Indian families and participated in their family activity. Each week we were asked to speak to Indian groups concerning our personal responsibilities in the U.S. At the time, Watergate was the chief interest. I had to explain our system of government as to how we handled a situation contained in Watergate.

Upon my return from India, I began dating my best friend Cindy, whom I asked to marry me. We have three children who have given us four grandchildren: three boys and one girl. Shortly after our marriage, I was hired by Motorola Communications and Electronics Incorporated. I was responsible for sales within counties of Central and Northern New York State, designing, bidding, and installing communication systems to State and Local Police, Fire, EMS and government communities. I eventually was promoted to District Sales Manager for upstate New York. This included all counties from the Canadian border to the Pennsylvania and Western counties to the Ohio border. It was a very interesting business with sales of over five-million dollars.

I retired from Motorola in 1998 and drove a tour bus for two years leaving that job for one driving a school bus for West Genesee Central School District. I retired in 2012 from West Genesee after twelve years. We moved from Syracuse, New York to Anderson, South Carolina in 2014 and moved into our present home on September 15, 2015. I joined Vets Helping Vets Anderson in 2017.

Bob Robinson

My name is Robert Lewis Robinson. I was actually born in Naples, Italy on May the 10th. My father was a submariner and a weapons officer on the USS Lionfish. The USS Lionfish was used in WWII and is now moored in Battleship Cove, Fall River, Massachusetts.

We were in the middle of the Cold War. At that point, they were hiding the submarines so that no one would know the location of the submarines. They did everything possible to keep it from ever being known that the officers could take their wives and family to where they were stationed. They did not allow any correspondence about dependents. A Certificate of Live Birth was issued when I was born. My parents were told they would be issued a birth certificate for me when they returned to their duty station in Portsmouth, Virginia.

One year later, we returned to Dad's duty station. The year was 1950 which is what they printed as my birth year. We went straight to Guantanamo Bay, Cuba and that is where my brother was born. Mom received both birth certificates so our orders could be cut to go with Dad for his duty in Hawaii. That is when she noticed that the date was wrong. She had lost the Certificate of Live Birth and decided to let it be. I am actually a year older than my so called birthdate.

By the time my father retired after twenty-six years of service, we had moved every four to six months. Mother kept all our stuff in a trunk that could be transferred in a moment's notice, which was pretty much the amount of time we had between transfers. We would find out one day and the next day we were traveling. She had one trunk for my brother and me, and one trunk for her things. All we would pack was personal items and the Navy would ship the trunks to us in a couple of days.

My dad was Golden Pate Robinson. He was born in Atlanta, Georgia and raised in Lawrenceville. He met my mom when he was taking my uncle Joe home. Uncle Joe was a machinist on the USS Lionfish with my father. Dad met Mom and knew he wanted to someday marry her. Uncle Joe never had a problem catching a ride home from then on.

Back to my birth certificate. The Army required me to have a top secret clearance. While they were checking, the FBI agent came by to see me and told me he was having a terrible time. Because of the frequent moves my family made, I attended twenty-six different schools and that included kindergarten in Hawaii. I happened to have my father's pay records and was able to give him the information so he could go back and find out exactly where we were at any given time.

I remember most vividly my dad being a great officer. When we would go to the ship and he would be getting ready to ship out, I had the run of the ship. It was a real treat. Going back to visit the USS Lionfish, I knew exactly where everything was, his bunk, desk, and Battle stations.

My younger brother joined the Army as well, but he got injured during AIT and was medically released. My brother Gregory Pete Robinson died in 2002. We lived an interesting life.

After Dad retired, he went to work with the ROTC program at Clemson University. He was also part-owner in the Poinsett Hotel in Greenville, South Carolina. At that time, we lived on Washington Street. Walking distance to the Poinsette and Cleveland Park. Dad would tell us to come up there and we would take off walking. We got to meet many interesting celebrities when they would come through doing some kind of promotional event.

One time I got to ride a saddled horse up to where they were keeping Trigger, Roy Roger's horse. I met Clayton Powell, the Lone Ranger, and Joe Lewis, the boxer. While I was training in San Antonia, Texas, John Wayne was filming a movie. I was in uniform, and he came over to talk to me. He was a big guy about my size except for the middle. I did not have a middle!

I left high school early to enlist in 1968. I had already completed all the credits I needed to graduate so they released me to go into the Army. I was living at 213 Willow Springs Drive in Clemson, South Carolina.

After attending basic training at Fort Jackson, South Carolina, I went on to AIT in eastern Texas. I knew exactly what I was going to do because I had already been taking classes, received all the first aid certifications, and became an Emergency Medical Technician, as it is called now.

I also knew I was going to become a Paratrooper. I went to jump school at Fort Benning, Georgia right after AIT where most people went directly to Vietnam. For some odd reason when it came down to going as a replacement for the 173rd Airborne Brigade, something got put off. They sent me to Germany, instead.

About three and half months later, they woke me up at 2:00 o'clock in the morning, told me to report to the Orderly Room with just my boots, my fatigue pants, a T-shirt with dog tags hanging out of shirt, and an extra pair of socks in my pocket. I knew what it was for; I had been selected to go to Wiesbaden Air Base. We were issued our uniforms on the plane going to Vietnam as replacements for the 173rd Airborne Brigade.

I have seven years of service. I did two tours in Vietnam and made several other trips. I was wounded twice. I was awarded my Purple Heart when I was shot in the arm, and it came out through my right hand. I received a Bronze Star, Army Commendation Medal, Air Medal, a Major Cross for Gallantry with Palm Leaf. My most suspicious one is the Good Conduct Medal.

When I got to Vietnam in the latter part of '68 and '69, the news coverage had pretty much prepared me for what to expect. I guess the Vietnam War was the first conflict that was covered every day on the news. The thing that surprised me the most was how hot it was and how bad it smelled. Being a combat medic, I was out working at company level as an infantryman until someone was injured. Then I became a medic. The 173rd Airborne stayed in the field constantly. Although, we had the Headquarters company where our surgeon manned a little aid station with four or five guys.

One of the most memorable guy was a fellow by the name of Joe Frazier. He was a black fellow about five foot ten or eleven inches. Real round shoulder muscular guy that was missing one tooth. He looked like Joe Frazier, and I will never forget that he was from Brooklyn, New York, and he kept telling me that when we get out of here I want you to go to New York with me. We are going to become cops up there. I kept telling Joe that I had no reason to go to New York.

The memorable part, he was the first person I met in country. I got there a little after noon and Joe said you might as well go with me tonight. We are going on ambush. Come on in here and we will pack you light to get you ready to go. So, the first night I went out with ambush patrol and was fired at. I started off shooting on full-automatic and had gotten about two magazines out when Joe told me not to do that anymore. He said that we did not have enough bullets. Good advice, but a wakeup call. Later Joe was severely wounded and died before making it out of country.

In these situations, training and paying attention increases your chance of having what is known as good luck. I had a good sense of humor, but I did not pull anything on anyone. I always try to stay sober and to this day have never smoked a marijuana cigarette or taken any kind of drug. I did not drink to excess at any time.

When I came home from Vietnam the first time, I had to go through Los Angeles International Airport (LAX). A group of Hare Krishna's were protesting with shaved heads, wearing monk like clothing. It was not the welcome home one would expect. That was their right, but I was appalled because I had just spent nine months and four days in the field at Vietnam. We did not have a say in anything. The only thing we lived for was to keep ourselves and our buddy alive.

I left the military in 1975 and was sick for years with stomach issues. I should have been dead from what I have heard. I went to work for the Veterans Administration in Lake City, Florida running their Emergency Room as a Triage Officer and worked in the emergency room with the patients coming in. After having my stomach removed entirely, I never fully recovered.

At one point in my military career, I looked like my nick name, "Little Abner." I was six foot three inches tall and weighed about two hundred sixty pounds. I had a fifty four inch chest and a thirty inch waist. It was a challenge trying to get a uniform that did not pull at the top or looked like I was pregnant at the bottom.

I went to North Carolina to be close to a VA facility because I was having problems with my health at this time. Then I went to the University of North Carolina in Ashville for general studies. I did not choose a major until I went to the second portion which was at the University of South Carolina in Colombia. Again, choosing to be close to a VA facility. I took Industrial Management, and my degree reads Interdisciplinary Studies. I wanted a general education, so I took the things that interested me, and I only liked a couple of credits being a meteorologist. Everybody talks about the weather so you might as well have some intelligence about it.

The thing I miss the most about the military was the structure. You knew what you were going to wear, where you were going to be, and you had something different to do every day. I had good camaraderie with my friends and the people who were under me. I was raised in a military family on Navy bases, and I never thought I would do anything but serve in the military.

I had the unique ability to adapt in tough situations when others found it hard, instead of panicking, I remained calm. I was able to function at a high level no matter what the situation was around me. That may be a learned response, or it could be inborn. I just do not think I can take credit for my responses; it was inborn. I wish I could ball it up and give it to some of the people. When things are happening, people get really excited, and a lot of adrenaline comes. I have only had a couple of times the adrenaline rush hit me. Later, I wondered what triggered that response.

Some advice that I practice myself that would help the young people of today is if you are asked to do something, do not see the negatives behind it; show the willingness to try. I always give a request a good airborne try. If you say yes, mean yes. Do everything you can to begin and finish the task.

My first daughter was born at Fort Bragg, North Carolina, the second daughter was born in South Carolina and the third was born when I was in the VA system down in Florida. The youngest one was my fishing buddy, getting up at 4:30 in the morning to go fishing with me. She died this past year at forty-five. She went to sleep by herself and woke up with Jesus.

I met my wife Fredda, down in Calhoun Falls, in 1968. Life and distance came between us. I went one way, and she stayed put. We were fortunate to meet again and have been married for ten years.

I was introduced to Vets Helping Vets Anderson by Billy Arflin who has now passed. Up until that point you might say that I had crawled into my shell, and nobody knew who I was or where I came from except that I was retired. I did not get out much. VHVA opened up a whole new world of service. I was back with friends and brothers that had been there and had the same mindset. Now we serve together on a new mission helping other vets.

Retiring from the medical field, I used my knowledge and headed up providing medical equipment and other supplies. I also have helped as a caretaker's helping hand. Our group lets you serve wherever your particular skill level or interest is needed. Something that might have been put on the back burner, may help you become a better person through VHVA.

Ronnie Roper

My name is Ronald Eugene Roper, and I was the second of seven children. After graduation in 1967 from T.L. Hanna High School in Anderson, South Carolina. I was drifting with no purpose in life.

I was classified as 1-A by the draft board and because of that classification the possibilities for getting a job were very slim. I went to the draft board in Anderson in December of 1968 to find out when I might be drafted and was told probably May or June. I asked if I could volunteer. The lady there said absolutely. So, I did. Less than a week later I received my notice to report to Fort Jackson, South Carolina on January 13, 1969.

It was a cold, rainy morning when I reported to the Anderson Post Office to take a bus down to Fort Jackson. Because of the weather and already having a sore throat before I left, I spent my first week in the hospital for strep throat. I did manage to get my "haircut" which I believed helped with the strep throat I developed. Standing in line, outside with a fresh haircut, I managed to get all my equipment to carry around that day. I was still at the Reception Station when I went to the hospital. It was quite an ordeal getting there, and I knew the next two years would be really trying.

I did my basic training with the guys I came in with, and after graduation as we were in formation, awaiting our Military Occupational Specialties (MOS) assignment. I figured since I was drafted that I would be 11-B-10 Infantry.

When they called out my name, it was 12-B-10, and I was going to Fort Leonard Wood Missouri for AIT. I was going to be a Combat Engineer. We learned about bridges, minesweeping, demolitions, and tying knots.

Upon graduation, I received orders to Vietnam, which was not unexpected. I expected that it was where I would go from the time I volunteered for the draft. I arrived on June 13, 1969, and turned nineteen on the 26th of June. I was assigned to Company C, 1st Engineer Battalion, 1st Infantry Division. Our area of operation was in the 3 corps area around Saigon. Our duties included mine sweeps, land clearing, fire base construction to include perimeter fencing and drainage, clearing land zones, reinforcing TOC bunkers as well as running communication lines, and other details as needed. We were often assigned to infantry units where we were on patrol in case undetonated bombs were found, or tunnels. Being a Combat Engineer, we were often called to explore tunnels for any sign of activity, and afterwards we would destroy them with explosives. We were the tunnel rats when required, security when needed and handled body counts and removal due to booby trap danger.

Upon successful completion of one year, we returned home to a hostile nation. All Vietnam veterans were held responsible for what was conceived as killing of civilians and babies, promoted by the radical protesters, especially in the parts of the country where Vietnam veterans were returned to the United States. I came back to Fort Lewis, Washington. We were told not to wear our uniforms to the Seattle-Tacoma

Airport because of constant protest by these people targeting returning veterans.

I had five months remaining and was assigned to Fort Hood, Texas to the 1st Armored Division. Time there was peaceful, and I played in a country music band most of the time I was there. It was a good five months, although I spent about every evening drinking, trying to remove the last year from my memory. After separation from service in 1971, I returned to Anderson, South Carolina to continue my life there as a civilian. I was proud to have served and glad I was one of the lucky ones to return. But it was not that easy to transition, as the friends I had known two years before were married, or still trying to determine their future.

I got married soon after returning and we had a daughter that died at childbirth. A couple years later, we had another one who was the apple of my eye. I was still struggling with my past in the military and continued to drink and work all the time. I enrolled in night school at Anderson College and graduated there with an associate degree in management and continued to Limestone College to graduate with a BS degree in management science.

Because my working full time and going to school at night my marriage was beginning to become strained and finally ended in divorce. I blame myself because of the activities I got involved with still trying to understand myself and where I fit in. I remarried about two years later and it was good at first, but depression seemed to follow me into marriage as well. Looking back, I can see how difficult it was for both of them to live with me. Although I had lots of friends, I had no one to talk to that would understand what I was dealing with.

I found Vets Helping Vets Anderson through a longtime friend who invited me to attend their meetings. This is what I had longed for, people who had been there and understood without judgement. That was in October 2016. My wife committed suicide in October 2017 because of drug addiction and depression that I still feel responsible for.

This group has been my salvation, making me feel worthy of being accepted and without this group I would have returned to the deep guilt and depression I had felt for so long. I am now involved with some of the best people I have ever known. I have finally accepted my past and I am trying to move forward with who I am. I appreciate the opportunity to put my story writing. This group has saved my life and given me the opportunity to give back to other veterans in our community. Thanks to all involved with sharing their stories and putting this book together so we are not forgotten.

William Sarge Sanchez

Born in 1930 and the Bronx, my childhood was probably different from most. I was placed in a foster home shortly after birth to escape an abusive alcoholic father. The Davila family raised me as their own in Spanish Harlem, but it was the Depression and times were tough. When circumstances became especially dire, I was placed Saint Agnes' Orphanage.

Some of my most vivid memories of that time include kneeling on a bed of gravel to say prayers to a statue of the Virgin Mary, being sent out as cheap child labor o pick tomatoes and being whipped for infractions.

I was glad to return home to my family after several years. It was only after I asked my mom for my birth certificate so I could enlist that I was told my name was not Davila, but Sanchez. I met my birth mother briefly and moved on with my life.

So, I enlisted at seventeen in 1947 and found myself at Fort Dix in New Jersey where I was trained to drive trucks. Next stop Korea, where I served from 1950 to 1953, driving trucks and helping to build roads. I had never been so cold in my life. After Korea, I was stationed in White Sands, New Mexico where I was the driver for Werner von Braun, an aerospace engineer and space architect.

By this time, I had decided to make the Army my career. There was nothing for me in New York and the pay was good. My next posting was Fort Niagara where I met my wife Bertha in 1955. During my time in the service, I played football for the Army at Fort Dix, and spent time in Germany as a supply Sergeant. Then back to the states at Fort Benning where I trained as a paratrooper, and then finally to Alaska where I retired after twenty-two plus years in 1969. Along the way, Bertha and I had four kids.

Now it was time to decide where to settle down with the family. Big cities held no appeal for me, so when an army buddy by the name of J. C. Schubert Suggested his hometown, we thought why not? Anderson, South Carolina became our home. I worked at Mary Carter Paints, then managed the Hess station downtown. As an early supporter of the Coleman Rec Center, I was an umpire for just about every sport. In 1983, I retired but continued as an umpire. Bertha and I have nine grandkids and fourteen great-grandkids. I have been a member of Saint George's Episcopal Church since its beginning. I am part of Veterans Helping Veterans Anderson for the camaraderie and because I enjoy helping others.

Lee Simon

I am a second-generation Naval Officer. My father was a CWO-4 Medical Service Corps (MSC) who had enlisted in 1935 from Anderson, Indiana. He went through boot camp at Norfolk, Virginia. After completion of initial medical training, he served as an Operating Room tech at nearby Portsmouth, Naval Hospital. He went to sea aboard USS Yorktown (CV-5) which was an aircraft carrier homeported in Norfolk. In November 1941, he raced home to South Gate, California, on emergency leave as his mother was about to pass away. He was still in California on December 7,1941. He hurriedly returned to Norfolk to rejoin USS Yorktown. But during the chaos in December 1941, he was grabbed in Norfolk for a special project. The project went well and then he was sent to Great Lakes, Illinois to help start a new Hospital Corps School. He volunteered for submarine duty and was part of the commission crew of the USS Tunny (SS-282). He made four combat war patrols as the Tunny's one-man medical department. He became too senior to remain aboard the Tunny. He was again assigned to the Hospital Corps School in Great Lakes where he married my mother in 1944. He was commissioned on 19 February 1947 and retired in 1964

In March 1947, I was born in the Long Beach Naval Hospital (in route to Guam). I was an only child and as a Navy family we moved regularly. From Guam we moved to Brooklyn, New York, to Great Lakes, Illinois, to Alameda, California, to Corpus Christi, Texas, to Orange, Texas, to

Taipei, Taiwan (when it was Nationalist China) and finally to San Leandro, California where my father retired. Our shortest move was from Corpus Christi to Orange, Texas. My freshman high school year was in Taiwan, after which, we returned to California where I graduated from San Lorenzo High School. In California, I worked Saturdays in my grandparents' launderette. At high school graduation, I looked forward to going to University of California, Berkeley, earning a degree in Civil Engineering, and starting a career in the Navy.

Vietnam went from an occasional obscure news story to nightly headlines between my high school graduation in 1965 and my college graduation in 1969. When I graduated from high school a few of us knew that the Mekong Delta existed. By the time I graduated from college, many of my high school classmates had been killed and almost everybody had been seeing too much of Vietnam on the 6 o'clock news. In Spring 1969, I applied for the 2-year NROTC program at UC Berkeley so that I could earn a master's degree in Sanitary Engineering (a hybrid of Public Health and Civil Engineering). My two-year Naval Reserve (NROTC) "boot camp" was a Summer at UCLA catching up with the regular four-year NROTC cohort. Following success at UCLA, I was inducted into the NROTC at Cal in October 1969. In the Summer of 1970, the USS Sutter County (LST-1070) was surprised to find two midshipmen wonder up from the beach in Vung Tau, Vietnam, for training. The USS Sutter County thought they had seen the last of the midshipmen when they left Japan enroute to Vietnam. The Commanding Officer told us not to get killed because he did not want to figure out how to do the paperwork. We promised to try not to be an administrative burden. My father passed away while I was at sea on the USS Sutter County in transit from Da Nang, Vietnam to Guam.

I returned to US Berkeley and was commissioned as a regular Navy (USN vice USNR) Civil Engineer Corps (CEC) Ensign (O-1) on 4 January 1971. On 13 February 1971, I married Judy, who I met at UCLA in 1969. We have three children and five grandchildren. One of our children and her family settled in Anderson in 2011. Judy and I escaped California in April 2021 and are loving retirement here in Anderson. Upstate is much like California was in the golden years before Vietnam as opposed to the crazy place that we have seen California become in the 21st Century.

After a quick honeymoon, I reported to Civil Engineer Corps Officers School (CECOS) in Port Hueneme, California for specialty training. At CECOS, we were asked to write career goals, so I put down a respectably ambitious set of goals for a 20-year career. I wanted to be a Public Works Officer, a Contracting Officer (ROICC/AROICC), command Seabees, and be President of a SAME Post (e.g., the leader of a local chapter of the engineering society all CEC officers were supposed to join). Little did I know that Providence would intervene, and I'd achieve these goals in the first four years of my CEC career.

At CECOS I asked the assignment officer to make me an independent Public Works Officer (PWO). The assignment officer orally patted me on the head and told me that the CEC did not normally make an Ensign a PWO. I didn't know then that in the CEC community, visibility near the flagpole is the key to success. I had grown up around Hospital Corpsmen and in the Navy medical community independent duty garnered respect.

Providence intervened: a spot needed to be filled urgently at a Naval Hospital in North Carolina and suddenly I was assigned to be an independent PWO. My first duty station was as PWO, Naval Hospital Camp Lejeune, North Carolina and a contracting officer, e.g.: Resident/Assistant Resident Officer-In-Charge of Construction (ROICC/AROICC) for projects at the hospital. I had the opportunity to manage the planning and design of the new Main Operating Suite (MOR) as PWO. Then as AROICC, I supervised the MOR construction contract, and later as PWO I got to accept the MOR as the customer's representative. Navy medicine liked this 'conflict of interest' as the CEC now calls it because one might argue under which hat something went wrong but there was no doubt who wore the hat if something actually went wrong.

I felt my mission at the hospital was to use my engineering skills to optimize patient care rather than to impress other engineers or optimize the efficiency of my Public Works department. This caused me to work closely with the head OR nurse (an O-5) during the MOR project and another Nurse Corps O-5 who was responsible for all the wards. This patient care optimization approach later biased many of my decisions as we took Naval Hospital Camp Lejeune from a Naval Hospital (e.g., 500 beds) to a Naval

Regional Medical Center (e.g., a 500 bed hospital, a 50 bed hospital miles away at Cherry Point, North Carolina and seven local satellite clinics).

After two and a half years at Camp Lejeune, my next duty station was command of a Seabee unit (Officer-In-Charge, NCBU 401 Great Lakes, Illinois). This was normally a prized second assignment following a very successful first assignment with a Seabee battalion. Assignment to command of a NCBU was unusual because had to be approved by the NCBU Program Manager in the engineer headquarters (NAVFAC) before the assignment officer in the personnel headquarters (BUPERS) could make the assignment.

Providence had intervened again: after a non-Seabee first assignment I had been offered command of NCBU 401. On the way from Camp Lejeune to Great Lakes, my orders had me stop at both BUPERS and NAVFAC in Washington DC. Out of curiosity, I had to ask the NCBU Program Manager how I got his approval as I had never met him. It turned out that the Nurse Corps Captain (O-6) from Camp Lejeune had been the President of the Nurse Corps Lieutenant (O-3) selection board. The NCBU Program Manager (a CEC O-4) was the 'disinterested recorder' of that selection board and for two weeks he had heard how good I was. This came as a complete surprise to me since I had very few of my interactions with the Nurse Corps Captain.

I had a successful two and a half years in command of NCBU 401. I saw the key to my mission was not to optimize construction project efficiency but rather to optimize construction project training value inherent in each project. If we had just done a steel project rather than seek a follow-on project that we could do again in steel, I would look for a follow-on project that we could do in concrete. While at Great Lakes, I saw that the closest SAME Post was 50 miles away which meant that a luncheon meeting in downtown Chicago basically killed the better part of a whole day. Having watched a SAME Post formed at Camp Lejeune, I showed the local engineers how to form a SAME Post at Great Lakes and was elected President once we got our charter. I wasn't really sure what to do with the post once it was formed. Providence was kind again and a local Army Corps of Engineers Brigadier General reached out to me after the Executive Director of SAME had surprised him with a congratulatory note. I had not bothered to tell the Brigadier that I was forming a SAME Post. He requested my presence for a meeting. Rather merely a 'grip & grin' courtesy call, he provided practical tips from what he learned as a SAME Post president in Seattle.

After two successful assignments, having completed all four of my twenty-year goals, and having a sick mother-in-law in living near the big Seabee base in Southern California, I was requested any type assignment at any location the Central, Mountain, or Pacific time zones. Naturally, the Navy sent me to Philadelphia, Pennsylvania where I spent the required one year minimum. Philadelphia was interesting. I had less facilities money to support the base for five quarters than my predecessor had for the previous four quarters. I had less money to spend on ground maintenance than one tenant spent on indoor office plants. The great challenge was my big neighbor who provided

247

maintenance on a reimbursable basis tended to treat symptoms rather than the underlying problem. A hypothetical sign might read: "Ok if the green light is on, call Maintenance if red light is on…" Unfortunately, if the red light came on, Maintenance would arrive, and switch lens covers problem solved by making the red light become the green.

After one year in Philadelphia, I resigned my LT CEC USN (O-3) commission effective 30 June 19 77, I was commissioned a LTJG MSC USNR (O-2) on 1 July 1977. In mid-July 1977, I reported to 1st Medical Battalion on Marine Corps Base, Camp Pendleton, California, and led its Preventive Medicine Section supporting 40,000 deployable Marines. The Public Health portion of my Sanitary Engineering education was the basis for USNR commission but my experience at Camp Pendleton was professionally rewarding as well as sometimes humorous and colorful. I left active duty 0n 30 May 1980 and made my home in San Diego, California, until I moved to Anderson in 2021.

I was a weekend warrior with USMCR Medical, Naval Air Reserve, USMCR Civil Affairs and surface USNR units. Civil Affairs was referred to as the softer kinder part of Special Operations. In April 1999, I was invited to return to active duty with the I Marine Expeditionary Force (MEF), G-3 Future Ops section (Camp Pendleton, California). My military and civilian background looked as though Providence had tailored my experience for Consequence Management (CM) e.g., mitigating the effects of a CBRNE accident/incident. As a Navy civil servant, I had been using large contracts for environmental cleanups. I had extensive

USMCR experience including USMCR Civil Affairs and USMCR command as well as Public Health training and experience. At the MEF, my skills were utilized in several CM exercises with both PACOM and CENTCOM. I helped train I Corps at Fort Lewis, Washington when it assumed the PACOM mission from the MEF.

On 9/11/2001, my plane was at the gate in San Diego waiting to go to Tampa, Florida (CENTCOM) for the initial planning conference for an exercise that would include CM. The plane was on extended gate hold, so we got off to wait in the airport. One tower was burning on the TV in the airport bar while we waited to reboard. Then we saw a plane hit the second tower. We headed back to the MEF at Camp Pendleton. Obviously, the exercise conference was cancelled. I shared CM planning templates with the I MEB (the brigade command element that comes out of the MEF command element) and provided quick refresher training on CM. The MEB was deploying to Egypt for Exercise Bright Star the four weeks. The MEF/MEB was the nucleus should CENTCOM need to form a JTM/CM.

In October 2001, I led a CM Augmentation Cell from I MEF to CENTCOM and helped form and launch Combined Joint Task Force Consequence Management (CJTF/CM) to Kuwait. "Combined" reflected the multi-national nature of CJTF/CM while the "Joint" refers to the fact that CJTF/CM was formed from more than one of the DOD military departments. Fortunately, no friendly or hostile nation needed a CM response. I visited CJTF/CM at Camp Doha, Kuwait, in the Summer of 2002 and saw that the Czechs were good (as a retired Special Forces Colonel had discovered during the first Gulf War). On 30 September 2002, I was released from active duty and retired effective 1 February 2003.

Looking back, Providence intervened in my father's and in my life's paths. Providence repeatedly placed each of us unexpectedly in the right place to meet some critical need. In hindsight, the unexpected frequently turned out to be a blessing, but it often didn't feel like a blessing at the time.

I was happily surprised when I first visited VHVA in late 2022. It was great to feel both the upbeat nature of the group and the 'small unit comradery' of VHVA.

Clay Sorensen

My name is Clayton D. Sorensen, and my nickname is Clay. I enlisted in the regular Navy in August of 1964 for four year active plus two year reserve obligation. At the time of my enlistment, I lived in Omaha, Nebraska.

I joined the Navy as a result of a disagreement with my dad. I was awarded a full college football scholarship, but after one year, chose not to pay much attention to my studies. When dad got on to me and I told him, "I would be better off joining the Navy." It was pretty much a bluff, but he called me out on it, and I would not back down. I chose the Navy because my uncle had been on a battleship during WWII, and I always looked up to him. Never considered any other branch of service.

After growing up on a farm in the Midwest, boot camp in San Diego was a cakewalk. The hours were similar to home and the work was much easier. I loved the warm weather and chances to meet people from all over the country.

A funny moment or maybe just unusual was my first "liberty" from boot camp in San Diego. My first time alone in a large city, especially a Navy city, and I had no idea what to do. Thinking back, I was pretty naive and dumb but had a great time anyway.

Adapting to Navy life was pretty easy. It was a four year adventure for me, learning great new electronic and nuclear trades, living on a large (Aircraft Carrier) ship and traveling all over the western United States and the West Pacific Ocean. I struggled a bit in dealing with authority (still do) but decided to make the most of it. I made a decision that as long as I was there, I was going to make the best of my time and I did. I studied hard, saved my money, got married, and attained the maximum allowable promotions. Life for me was good.

I enlisted just before the Vietnam War started and was actually on liberty in Hong Kong from my ship (USS Hancock CVA 19) when the Diem brothers, who were in charge of South Vietnam, were executed. We were pulled off liberty and went directly to duty off the coast of Vietnam in the South China Sea. I think this is pretty much recognized as the beginning of the war. Lots of stuff that did not make the news was going on secretly after that.

I completed electronics school at Great Lakes Naval Station after boot camp. Upon graduation, I spent a year in Nuclear Weapons School off Sandia Base in Albuquerque, New Mexico and became a Nuclear Weapons Technician. I also trained for Explosive Ordinance Demolition (EOD) and attended several electronic schools on North Island Naval Air station in San Diego, California. Long answer, I was a Nuclear Weapons Technician and an EOD technician on an aircraft carrier for the balance of my career. The "Nuclear Weapons Technician" rating name was later changed to "Gunners Mate Technician" to appease folks in Asia, especially Japan.

There are so many memorable things, good and bad to remember about my deployments. Seeing all the new places, people and countries was mind boggling for a farm kid from Nebraska. I made friends from all over and enjoyed the different cultures. There were beautiful beaches in Hawaii, Japan and Australia; Fantastic scenery and boat villages in Hong Kong; And crazy "jeepneys" in the Philippines. A jeepney was a crowed minibus used for public transportation decorated with spray painted designs.

All of the places had fun bars and clubs; lots of places for a dumb kid to spend his money. I did a good job of managing my money and was always a "lender" and not a "lendee" when we arrived in port. Also remember buying all sorts of china, crystal, and new suits while in many ports of call. I do remember seeing parts of the "Ugly Americans" too - in bars and in the way many Americans treated our foreign host. It was a lesson I carry with me to this day.

One of the more memorable happenings was the assassination of President John Kennedy on November 22, 1963. We were in the middle of the Pacific Ocean and had very little ways of communication. There were no Wi-Fi, cell phones, satellite phones, etc. We had somehow picked the news off AP wires and the rumors quickly circulated. All we knew was that he was killed by a guy with Soviet connections, and all thought we were going to war with Russia.

I did not see "face to face" combat but our ship was involved in bombing, photography, and scouting off the coast of Vietnam. There were casualties from planes being shot down, crashing when landing and/or taking off from the ship, and airplane and weapons handlers that were killed and injured on the ship. I do have a 30% PTSD partial disability rating, brought on I am told, by witnessing many of these incidents. We were also tasked and ordered to head "around the horn" to participate in the Cuban Missile Crisis. We were not allowed to tell our families where we were or where we were going. Luckily, the incident was terminated before we reported on station.

In addition to many months of school, I spent two and a half deployments to the western Pacific and the South China Sea off the coast of Vietnam. The deployments were fairly similar, but I was older, the next time around, and knew what to expect. The war was accelerating and many of my friends were getting extended for more duty. I often thought about that, but it did not come to pass. Since I was married, I spent more time aboard ship studying and generally trying to behave myself. I was fortunate enough not to become injured.

With the exception of the Good Conduct Medal, most every serviceman receives, the only other medal I received was the American Spirit Honor Medal as the most outstanding recruit in boot camp. I studied hard and did well and was granted the medal out of two thousand other recruits graduating. They flew my parents out to the graduation ceremony, and I think this was the proudest my dad had ever been.

The return home was strange and disappointing. I had taken an oath and pledged to do whatever was asked of me on behalf of my country. Being in a nuclear program, I even had to take regular psychological exams to make certain I was OK with the possibility of launching weapons that could do harm to thousands of people. I took it very seriously and was honored that my country trusted me with such a heavy responsibility. I had also learned to appreciate and missed the many benefits, comforts, and liberties we enjoyed and took for granted as Americans. I missed my country, and I was glad to be home.

Yeah upon returning I found that many people, mostly the ones who did not serve, blamed us for the war and the deaths of so many people. Many terrible things were said to us and about us. I did not blame my country, though I should have questioned our so-called leadership. I did not have time for the hypocrites and the idiots who taunted us.

There are many with whom I served and have fond memories. I befriended and became close to a young Ensign from Chicago on my first cruise. As time went on, he rose to a full Lieutenant. We talked often about making a career of the service but he (because of my question of motives and authority) advised that I should probably get out, finish college, and make my way in civilian life. I actually qualified for E6 and OCS, if I had "shipped over" but I took his advice and got out. I did go on to finish college and I'm forever grateful for his consul and friendship.

We had a good group of guys in our division and most of our activities, when we were in port, evolved around the water, beaches, and swimming. We even became acquainted with some Brits when we were in port in the Philippines, alongside HMS Ark Royal (British Aircraft Carrier). We quickly learned they, according to rank, were issued rations of rum, beer, etc. We enjoyed visiting their ship and sharing their rations.

There was not anything that I particularly did for good luck on departure. However, since our home port was

Alameda, California, in the Bay area, always made it a point to go topside when leaving and returning under the Golden Gate Bridge. It was my symbol of home, and it made the hair stand up on my back. I am certain that it still would.

In conclusion, I would say that my four years in the Navy were some of the best in my life. I never regretted being there when I was in, and I appreciate my time even more the older I get. I "grew up" in the service and have no idea what my life might be like today if I had chosen a different path.

Many friends were made, first-hand lessons learned about life and the world. I became a member of a "band of brothers" that will always be there and appreciate me no matter what branch, when or where we served. My dad was 4F during WWII and was rejected when he tried to join. He was also a dairy man and was considered in a critical position for the war effort. He told me many times growing up that the one thing he missed was the ability to hang with service buddies, tell war stories, and share the camaraderie that goes with it. I think that lesson from him was also one of the drivers for my enlistment.

Nothing demonstrates this thought better than Vets Helping Vets Anderson. I am honored and proud to be a part of the organization and I am still making new best friends to this day. It is also heartening to meet other vets in life, and just sharing a handshake and/or a knowing nod, maybe even a few stories. It is something earned and will always be treasured. That is my story, "in my own words."

Bob Steadman

I was born in Anderson, South Carolina, and have lived here all my life. I was raised in the Homeland Park area of South Anderson. My mom lived in the same house I was raised in until her passing in 2023. She had lived there for seventy-seven years. I attended Southside Elementary School, McCants Junior High School, and T.L. Hanna High School (the first year boys and girls attended together). I graduated in 1965. My childhood was a happy normal childhood, my family was poor, but we didn't know we were poor, because everyone we knew was in the same situation.

I began working at an early age in the Mail Room of the Daily Newspaper and did that through high school. My senior year I worked about thirty hours a week as well as attending school. I did not have immediate plans for college, so I opted to join the service, and hopefully receive training in a career field of my choosing. I joined the United States Army in August of 1965, less than two months after graduating from high school at age seventeen. I knew that as Vietnam was heating up, my chances of being drafted were very high.

Joining the Army was a great choice for me, it taught me many things, among them were self-discipline, responsibility, and a sense of duty. I took basic training at Fort Gordon, Georgia and AIT at Fort Leonard Wood, Missouri. I was trained as an Army Administrative Specialist. My next assignment was to Erlangen, Germany with the 35th Armored Brigade of the 4th Armored Division. Here I worked in

Operations and Intelligence of our Battalion headquarters. As there was a tremendous shortage of officers, and the need of staffing in the Vietnam escalation, I was offered the opportunity to attend Officer Candidate School. I passed the board and was assigned to OCS at Fort Lee, Virginia.

This was a very demanding school lasting six months and I graduated and was Commissioned in April of 1967. I was sent to Fort Irwin, California where I had many different assignments. Fort Irwin was a staging and training center for Artillery Units being sent to Vietnam. I became XO of a Supply and Services Company. This type of company supports troops in the field with Supplies, Laundry and Bath Services, Fuel, Ammo, and Graves Registration.

In our Garrison setting, our assignments were modified. Our Laundry and Bath Platoon along with the equipment was once sent to Idaho to support firefighters battling a massive forest fire. Our GR platoon was modified to be a burial unit to handle funerals in two Nevada counties including Las Vegas and three counties in Southern California, including San Bernardino County. We sometimes conducted two funerals a day. There were many servicemen who lost their lives in Vietnam during this time.

We also had much training in crowd and riot control, as many areas of the country were dealing with civil rights issues and war protests during the 1960s. Because of the Officer shortage, I had the opportunity to become a company commander for several months. I also was tasked with handling reports of survey, picking up and transporting prisoners, and as a defense counsel for Special Court Martial cases. We also had some notification duties to families of wounded or deceased soldiers. This duty was difficult.

My Vietnam tour assignment came in January of 1968. I was assigned to the 501st Field Depot in Korat, Thailand. Thailand was the home of several Air Bases from the B-52s, surveillance planes and fighter planes. The Army managed the Port in the South of the Country and the Depot at Korat where I was based. Probably 50,000 Air Force troops, but only about 5,000 Army troops. Our work was logistical support of whatever was needed. Lots of trucking of Ordinance Fuel and other supplies. My job there was as a Property Disposal Officer, basically the operation of a military junkyard.

We recover precious metals especially silver and copper from airplane batteries. We also recovered silver from the miles of film when it was burned. The massive amount of scrap metals like iron and aluminum were sold by the U.S. to approved buyers. We also issued things like used bunk mattresses and surplus equipment to some of our Asian allies. The depot employed several hundred local nationals, and I also was the paymaster every two weeks for the civilian workforce.

Thailand was a much safer place than Vietnam period we did not get shot at, which was a blessing, but many of the air crews were not so lucky. My final assignment was back to Fort Jackson, South Carolina as the Commissary Officer, basically the military store manager. My assignments were to account for the proceeds, get them safely to the finance office, and verify the deposits. I was offered a promotion to stay another year but declined and returned home. I was very blessed during my service years, I was never in harm's way as many of my brothers were, but I did my best to do whatever I was asked to do.

After my service years, I married Donna Rhodes, which was the best decision of my life. We had two wonderful daughters who now have families of their own. I began a career as a Building Contractor and as a Property Manager, which I did for over forty years. I have made many wonderful friends. I decided some sixty years ago to do my best to serve the Lord and my fellow man. One of the reasons I joined the American Legion is that it is an organization that is God centered and devoted to service to our country and community. I love my Lord and try to serve Him, and I love my Country and continue to serve with Post 14 of the American Legion and with Chapter 40 of the DAV in Anderson. I thank my Heavenly Father for all my blessings and all my fellow Veterans for their service.

Frank Sullivan

My name is Jesse Franklyn Sullivan. My mother always told me that she sent my birth certificate back three times to get them to spell my name correctly. She wanted my name spelled using a "y" in Franklyn. I suspect she chose the name because Franklin D. Roosevelt was serving as President of the United States in 1943, the year I was born. My father's name was Jesse. I decided I liked to be called Frank.

We were living in Alexandria, Virginia when I enlisted. I was seventeen and a half years old and did not appear to have any goals or purpose. You might say I was trying to find my niche in life. I went up to Fort Holabird, Maryland, the Armed Forces induction facility to enlist. There I received my written and physical examinations. They gave me a choice of two military occupation specialties. I asked for an explanation of their duties. The recruiter explained as part of an engineer unit, I would be constantly using a shovel and wheel barrel. As part of an armored unit, I would be using a machine gun, this sounded more exciting to me.

One of the funny things about basic training was I could not stay in step when marching. My platoon Sergeant would get in my ear and keep hollering "your left, your left" but my right heel kept hitting the pavement. I finally realized I was taking too long of a step, once I corrected this my marching was fine!

After basic at Fort Jackson, South Carolina, I left for my advanced individual training at Fort Knox, Kentucky, the U. S. Armored Training Center. From there I was sent to

South Korea and assigned as an Armored Intel Specialist. There I joined the 40th MED Tank Battalion as an Armored Scout. We were sitting on and patrolled the DMZ above the 38th parallel. I was a Private E-2, sort of a gung ho young boy when I got there. Some of the older guys grumbled about the time they spent there and how their time was about up. They tried to discourage me by spouting off that I would not make any rank there, but I did. My section Sergeant was a Korean War veteran who was a no-nonsense kind of guy. Somehow I got along with him out of respect and with what he taught me, I became a confident man and soldier. We got extended due to the Berlin Crisis that occurred in 1961, so I served a total of sixteen months in Korea.

I went back to Fort Knox and served in the Honor Armored Guard there. Our assignment was to spit and polish all equipment, line the runway, and wait on dignitaries to come into the airport. I attended the NCO Academy as a E-5 and graduated 29th out of a class of 100. It was there I learned the importance of Non-commissioned Officers and their leadership. I decided I was going to make a career out of the military and serve twenty or maybe even thirty years.

I received my orders to Bad Kissingen, Germany to join the armored cavalry regiments stationed at the Daley Barracks. Bad Kissingen is a German spa town in the Bavarian region. Our unit performed surveillance and patrolled the border for the three years I was stationed there. There was a 5-kilometer restricted zone that was off-limits to all U.S. personnel. One day while out on patrol, I saw an automobile in the restricted zone. When we went back to investigate, I found my Sergeant Major from Fort Knox, his friend and their two wives sightseeing on vacation. He said he did not realize he had strayed past the restricted zone, but I had to arrest him. We escorted his vehicle between two jeeps back to the headquarters to be interrogated for entering a restricted zone. He agreed that it was the correct thing to do.

While in Germany I watched military personnel land, and then receive orders within the next twenty-four hours to report to Vietnam. With the war heating up, they were needing armored scouts. I felt it was my duty to volunteer for a stent in Vietnam. In September of 1967, we landed in Vietnam by ship and immediately went on duty. I served as a Staff Sergeant E-6 and was assigned to B Troop, 1st Squadron, 1st Armored Calvary.

Our job was to go into an area and assist, find the enemy so they could be destroyed, and help bring our own dead or wounded out. We followed the construction team of Marines down dirt roads in the morning as they swept for explosive devices left by the enemy. Then gave them a ride back. There was no assigned place to sleep. Out in the field, some of us used ammo boxes.

I was awarded two Purple Hearts, a Combat Infantryman Badge, and a Silver Star through the mail, while in the Watson Army Hospital at Fort Dix, New Jersey. After showing it to the Senior Ward Clerk, he turned it over to the Senior Hospital Executive. From there it was sent to the Post Commanding General's Office. I was then awarded the Silver Star by a parade. The Silver Star is the third highest U. S.

Combat-only award. This is how the "Award of the Silver Star" reads on my printed orders dated 24 December 1967:

Staff Sergeant Jesse F. Sullivan awarded Silver Star. The gallantry in action against a hostile force on 9 November 1967 in the Republic of Vietnam. On that date, Staff Sergeant Sullivan was assigned as a vehicle commander on an armored cavalry assault vehicle with B Troop, 1st Squadron, 1st Calvary, engaged in an assault on fortified enemy positions. His suppressing fire allowed another track to maneuver into position to place fire on the same location. Another direct hit was made on Sergeant Sullivan's track which forced him and his crew to evacuate. After learning that the two radios in his burning track were keeping the platoon's network jammed, Sergeant Sullivan ran across the open rice paddy to the track and turned off the radios. Then, noticing some infantry men pinned down on his left flank, he mounted atop the vehicle to his machine gun and laid down a heavy base of fire so they could move into position. Sergeant Sullivan then gathered his crew's personal weapons and ran back across the open area to deliver the weapons to his men. When two infantry men were wounded, Sergeant Sullivan again ran back, through the intense hostile fire, to his track to cover their evacuation. Discovering that several infantry men in the immediate area were low on ammunition, he distributed ammunition from his track and again took up fire with his weapon to cover the extraction of the wounded. While firing Sergeant Sullivan was wounded by a burst of enemy fire and evacuated. Sergeant Sullivan's courageous actions in providing covering fire from a burning vehicle, filled with explosives, allowed both infantry and vehicles to advance upon the objective. Staff Sergeant Sullivan's unquestionable valor in close combat is in keeping with the highest traditions of the military service and reflects great credit upon himself, the Americal Division and the United States Army.

I spent a year in the Watson Army Hospital at Fort Dix, New Jersey. Their orthopedic surgeon fused my hand and arm back together at the wrist. I remember them asking me what I did before entering the military. I told them I was a mechanic. I always enjoyed working on hot rods and vintage cars. He said son that is something you will not be able to do with your injuries. I, Frank Sullivan, am here to tell you right now: Never take never for an answer. You might not do things the way you use to, but with willpower and determination, there is an excellent chance you will find another way to do them.

The military decided to medically retire me from active duty. I insisted, I planned to make the military my career. Eventually I was awarded the same benefits as a twenty-year veteran. I kept my can-do attitude and went to work.

After my father retired, he and my mother moved to Anderson where Mother was from. I soon followed for I knew they were getting up in age and may need my assistance.

Anderson, South Carolina is where I met my wife Brenda. She taught me how to be a great achiever and encouraged me that I could do whatever I set out to do. I worked at New Car Dealerships as a mechanic and service manager. Eventually, I became Parts and Service Director over seven New Car Dealerships for Century Dealer Services in the Greenville, South Carolina area. My wife and I owned and operated Foothills Import Automotive on N. Murry Avenue, Anderson, South Carolina. Artificial knuckles replaced arthritic joints along with other medical setbacks, yet I never gave up. Restoring automobiles like my 1955 Chevrolet two-door post still remains my favorite pastime.

When I entered civilian life again, there were not many people interested in a Vietnam War veteran. Sitting around the break room with a group of guys, the last thing they wanted to hear was about the war. It could have been the media who gave so much negative publicity. Maybe the fact that some would not have gone if they were called up. Patriotism is an important part of keeping America free. Pledging allegiance to one Nation under God reinforces that, yet it is left out of school assemblies today. I encourage young people to join the military. There are many positions that are support groups and not strictly combat within the branches of service.

I joined a group of Purple Heart recipients that included Sammy Lewis and Phil Harris. They invited me to Vets Helping Vets Anderson. I enjoy the fellowship and look forward to when we can meet in our new facility.

Mike Walker

My name is Carl Michael Walker, my mother called me Mike, so everybody else does. I volunteered for the draft in September of 1968 to protect myself from going to college. But then it did not work because I got an early out from Vietnam to go to college. I had failed five grades in school and graduated high school when I was twenty. The University of Georgia gave me a certificate for a high score on the SAT. I was no dummy, but just well... what?

You can factor in that both my parents were alcoholics. Anyway, I did not want to go to college and my best friend proceeded me into the Army and combat in Vietnam. I was living with my mother in Athens, Georgia. I finished my formal education with a master's from Columbia International University.

When you volunteer for the draft, they put you in the infantry. After two weeks in basic training, we learned we could yell out the window at new recruits (two weeks newer than us). We would yell at them to do push-ups, and they would fearfully comply. It was a distraction we enjoyed.

Then from Basic Training at Fort Benning, Georgia, I went to Advanced Individual Training (AIT) at Fort Polk, Louisiana. During one exercise my company commander was explaining the map grid to another recruit and using scratched illustrations in the dirt. I took a stick and crossed out his diagram and said, "Don't listen to that, it will just confuse you." And then I explained the grid system and how to use it.

The Company Commander said, "That is a better way to explain it."

Another time I happened to be with two shake and bake Noncommissioned Officers (NCOs) looking at a map. One of them, Bob, questioned a map feature, the use of merging contour lines. I told him that indicated a very steep incline, which of course it did. Later that day the three of us were walking back to our camp. I said, "I would like to go to NCO school so I could teach people." NCO sergeants were in short supply in Vietnam, and this was the source of so-called "shake and bake" sergeants. Bob said, "Walker, you couldn't teach anyone anything." I told him I had taught him that day how to read a map. The rest of our walk was silent.

I went to Noncommissioned Officers Candidate School for twelve weeks at Fort Benning, Georgia and earned the distinction of being a "shake and bake" sergeant. Then I went to Airborne Jump School, but I did not pass because my upper body strength was not strong enough. I would not say I was weak. However, I did end up getting a hugely important benefit. Those few weeks, relative to the time I entered Vietnam in such a way that I was eligible for the maximum early out for college, based on the end of my enlistment. Oh, Happy Day! I discovered this towards the end of my tour in Vietnam. My mother searched for a college with the earliest matriculation date in Georgia, and I went home a few months early.

After being in country just a few weeks, my platoon was doing a sweep of what we thought was a deserted enemy bunker system. We walked into an ambush. They opened up on us with multiple machine guns. I could see the leaves fluttering and smoke from a machine gun nest. We carried (LAW) personal anti-tank rockets (like a single use Bazooka). One of our men called for suppressing fire and fired a LAW right down the source of the smoke. In just a few seconds, after the LAW exploded, the enemy's machine gun fire resumed. We were pinned down for hours. We continued the battle, passing machine gun ammo to our machine Gunners and passing LAW to the men in position to use them. Other platoons behind us passed their LAW forward to us. We provided suppressing fire when it was called for and firing LAW after LAW into their position.

My thought is as soon as one enemy crew was blown up they brought another machine gun into the bunker and started again. Finally, the decision was made to withdraw. Some risked their lives to retrieve our dead and wounded. They told us later that there was a battalion size unit of North Vietnamese Army (NVA) regulars to the west of our position.

Cobra gunships arrived and began showering lead and rockets in that direction. And then jets came with rockets and bombs. And then Puff the Magic Dragon came and lit up the evening as it was getting dark. Out of twenty-seven men, I was one of seven that remained, Nine were killed and eleven wounded. After that day, for the rest of my tour, my job was staying alive and returning home honorably. I was not committed to the war effort.

We did not have good platoon commanders, in my opinion. I do not think I ever had an encounter with officers at any level that caused me to respect them or their ability. I should remember, as a shake and bake, I did not really know what I was doing a lot of the times and made a lot of mistakes. The lieutenants were college ROTC graduates for the most part, so I should cut them some slack.

We spent a lot of time on extended backpacking camping trips in beautiful country. We had encounters with tigers, wild deer, and footlong centipedes. Our so called Kit Carson Scout was a Vietnamese scout who traveled with us. I understand he had been Vietcong soldier. Once a member of my squad told me he could not put on his rucksack because it had a caterpillar in it. I had never heard of such a thing. I told him that was ridiculous, until he showed it to me. Our Kit Carson got very excited and fished a one foot long, one and a half inch wide very dangerous looking centipede out of a pocket of the rucksack. Kit Carson cut the centipede in half and then we watched the two halves fight. It was hilariously funny to us.

We also had encounters with big brown one inch termites that bit. Sometimes we would be digging a hole to sleep in, to keep a low profile; and dig into a termite nest. The remedy was to find a few big inch and a half black ants and throw them into the swarming termites. The termites would evacuate, and you did not have to start a new hole. If you dug into a black ant nest the only remedy was a hammock or a new hole.

We also had leeches of an uncommon variety. They walked on the ground as well as lived in the creeks and rivers we waded through. I spent most of my in country time in the Central Highlands around Pleiku. Often after we crossed a river, we would have bloodstains above our belts and above the tops of our boots. Because the leeches would gorge themselves on our blood and fall off, only be crushed by the tight areas of our clothes as we moved. I was watching a leech walk down the trail following the heat of my body. It was a monopod, odd to watch as it inched along. I threw a lit cigarette near it and watched as the leech turned and tried to attack the burning end. I could hear the sizzle as the mouth of the leech latched onto the burning coal. I had shivers when I contemplated sleeping on the ground and decided to sleep in a hammock that night.

In my unit the sergeants (the squad leaders like me) took the responsibility to walk point. I do not know why; it is just the way it was. I was excellent with maps but had no sense of direction, and I still do not. I was quickly uninvited to walk point. One day I was number three behind point. (Moving through the jungle and open areas we walked single file. The most dangerous position was point man, the first man in the column.) Point man stepped up on something and then stepped up to walk across on a fallen log. Number two man came to the spot and backed up and walked around it. But usually, you stepped right where the man in front of you stepped. I objected, "Hey, why didn't you step where he stepped?" He replied, "There is a snake." I said, "Snake ain't gonna hurt you." By this time, I was up to the stepping up place. Point man had stepped on a large pile of reticulated Python lying in the underbrush. I made a detour, too. Number four man objected the same way I had, telling me the snake would not hurt me. I watched as he arrived at big snake stepping spot and he made a detour. I said, "Hey, man get back over there, snake ain't gonna hurt you." We all laughed about it later.

We had camaraderie and we had tragedies. The blood of slain patriots stained my clothes as I carried corpses from the battlefield. I heard bullets singing their songs with the beauty of a violent death. Something inside my soul shrank and withered.

When I left country, I noticed I had been awarded a Bronze Star, to this day, I do not know why. The certificate was just in my folder, and I do not remember reading it. I also had an Air Medal and a Combat Infantry Badge.

I had a lot of adventures. I returned home a changed person. Before I had sandbagged my vocabulary, and tried to act like I was not totally ignorant, and unconcerned with sports on TV. My hair grew longer, and my clothes became outlandish. I quit drinking and smoking pot; I had been a big drinker since around fourteen. I mean I quit getting drunk. After a year or so, I quit smoking and quit being predatory towards women. The war had broken something inside me, but I cannot define it. I am sure I had PTSD for at least six years. I became very political and wanted to change the world. I made speeches, I marched, I did sit-ins, and I got arrested. I threw my guns down a well and got a pacifist discharge from the inactive reserves. (The pacifist discharge involved trips to Atlanta from Athens, Georgia and interviews with chaplains that tried to talk me out of it. It did not change my honorable discharge. It took a lot of effort. And I am no longer a pacifist.)

After a year or more of being very political and two years after Vietnam, I was handing out leaflets on a street corner in Athens, Georgia. Looking back, I can understand why people might avoid a WILD looking hippie. I did not do drugs but probably looked like it. We were not a well-funded organization. I asked a friend of mine where we got the paper to print all these leaflets. He was proud of it, and he said, "We stole it from the University of Georgia." At that moment I realized that me and the people I was with were just as manipulative and self-serving as the ideologs we opposed.

I thought, if not politics: what? I stood there puzzled, looking for an anchor, looking for something solid to make sense of the world. I came to a conclusion. There needed to be more love in the world. People need to love each other more. Uh oh, I was under the microscope of my own soul. I NEEDED to change, I NEEDED to become a different person. I needed to love people more. I felt totally unable to achieve this new standard.

I would need God's help, but I did not know who God was. I firmly rejected the churchianity of my parents and the shallow religion I had experienced in the Army. The chaplains I had encountered and the memorial services I went to in Vietnam were shallow and without substance.

I would search for God. I wanted to go to the source material, not someone's opinion. We do not have to agree to be friends. I am not right about everything, and I am not the moral arbiter of other people's beliefs or behaviors. I like a good discussion. I have logical and articulate (well, to me at least) reasons for my conclusions and I am happy to listen to others. I explored every religion I encountered for a year or more: some organized, some cults, eastern religion, and western religions. I examined more religious expressions than most people could name.

One night in a stairwell of the University of Georgia, two guys from Bob Jones University talked to me. They were probably as skeptical of me as I was of them. They gave me a newsprint King James Bible, absolutely the cheapest made book I had ever seen. I had a shelf with the religious books that I had explored, maybe twenty books. I thought, I had read all this other stuff, so I will read this. I started with Matthew (I am glad they did not give me the Old Testament). Matthew 7:7 struck me: *Ask and it will be given to you; seek and you will find; knock and the door will be open to you.*

That struck me as what the real God would say. The more I read the more I felt like this was God opening the curtains and letting the light in. I surrendered to this Jesus. I had an experience described in Romans eight up to verse eighteen but particularly verse nine.

But I was still suffering from PTSD. A girl, an art major, asked me why I was so bitter. I said Vietnam. She said I should not be bitter; I should praise God for Vietnam. That had to be the dumbest thing I had ever heard coming from the most naive person I had ever met. But as I sat in my apartment later I thought about it. Jesus could have kept me out of Vietnam, or He could have prevented Vietnam altogether. I talked to God about it. I told him I could think of no reason to praise Him for Vietnam. I felt God impressed on me (not audibly) that He would give me the faith if I would praise Him for Vietnam in faith. So, I sought to do that and felt real praise for Vietnam, no intellectual reason, just blind faith. At the same time, I felt a huge healing in my soul. I do not know exactly what happened, but I do know there was a great healing in my soul.

One thing I would like for people to know is that we should not fight any wars we do not have to win. And if we fight, we should fight to win as quickly and cheaply as possible. I feel there has been a lot of adventurism wars we should have stayed out of or fought to win and then leave.

I think my time in the military has enabled me to identify with others who have deep grief, to view them with a compassion that can listen without giving advice or saying some platitude to make myself feel better. It certainly put me more in touch with myself, not caring if I was popular or fit in.

In service I gained an attention to detail that served me well. I worked my way through Graduate School, paint contracting. My real estate clients bragged about my attention to detail to other agents. Before retirement at sixty-eight, I was a commercial roofing contractor, and attention to detail enabled me to get a lot of return customers with a good profit margin.

I would want my children to know I served honorably and today I am proud of my service and patriotism. I did not want my sons to enter the military, I told them it would kill me if they died in some adventurism, unnecessary or foolish conflict.

I would say there is still something wounded inside me from the war. I do not think it is a bad thing, it is just a part of me that is hard to describe. I heard someone at Vets Helping Vets say that for years they were reserved about telling anyone they were a Vietnam veteran. I certainly had a sense of…shame maybe about Vietnam, about being so foolish as to being part of it. I do not know how to put it. It was a waste, heartbreaking waste. I cried at the Vietnam Memorial at the Capitol. There is something healing about Vets Helping Vets. I am glad I can be part of something that looks after vets. I feel happy at the meetings. *Faith not Religion, religion judges and divides, faith loves and serves.*

Robert Waterman

My name is Robert Waterman. I was born in Hartford, Connecticut, July of 1941. When christened some years later, James became my middle name. I chose to enlist because my father was very abusive. My clothes were worn out, my shoes had cardboard soles. While in high school, I always had a job, but my father took every bit of it every week. I graduated from West Haven High School in 1959. The place I was working part time gave me a full time job. My grades were good enough to get into the two state colleges to which I applied. Lack of money left me with two choices. One keep working and take classes or enlist so I would not be drafted.

I was sworn into the Army in August 1959. I boarded the bus in New Haven, Connecticut, and arrived at Fort Dix, New Jersey. The bus stopped in front of where we were housed. The light went on and the doors opened. We got off the bus and lined up. A half hour later I had more clothes and shoes that I could carry in the big bag called a duffel bag. What a life! New clothes and shoes that fit, three meals a day, and all I had to do is follow the rules. It is hard to explain how it felt to look like everyone else, and not be the pauper in the class.

I enjoyed basic training period the instructors really wanted all of us to succeed. With a few exceptions, we did. I was a sharpshooter. During basic training at Fort Dix, New Jersey, I was called into the Captain's office. He had received notice that the Army wanted me to go to the Officers Training Course and come out a Lieutenant. I stuck with my plans to go to college. My discharge would be later, but that is why I enlisted.

The tests given by the military are quite revealing. When I finished basic, I went to Fort Sam Houston, Texas and became a medic. From there, I was assigned to an Army clinic in Frankfurt, Germany, to work the rest of my two and a half years until my discharge. I took x-rays and set trays up so the doctors had all the needed tools to take care of the next patient. This is where my thinking about the future was conceived. Doctor Quercin from California bought his own materials that were the latest quality and used them when repairing my teeth. I had never been to a dentist in my whole eighteen years. There was much to be taken care of.

He told me that I would be obligated to participate in the entertainment of the facility that the military constructed for the troops. I agreed to do it because I participated in my high school entertainment. In these days I found out I was blessed with a voice and could sing.

Two doctors and I came home on the same boat from Bremerhaven, Germany to New York. I teared up at the Statue of Liberty because I was so glad to be home and ready to go to the university. As an enlisted, the soldier's pay was a hundred and twenty-five dollars per month. I saved a hundred dollars and kept the twenty-five dollars to buy three cartons of cigarettes and other sundries.

I had good relations with the doctors, registered nurses, and a full bird commander. When notified we were on alert, I had to hop in the ambulance and drive to the motor pool, check out a truck, drive like a bat out of hades to pick up the Colonel, and get him promptly to the chosen safe zone.

In August of 1962, Colonel Fairchild went to the PX and bought all my medals. He offered me a fifteen hundred dollar bonus and then an E-5 if I would reenlist. I did not. I had three thousand dollars saved to get started with the next phase of my life.

My service gave me so much pride in myself, and it convinced me I was a man. I got a job as a second in responsibility at an insurance company in New Haven, Connecticut. I was soon the manager. It was simple accounting, and I supervised four ladies. After three years, I dated Carol. We later married.

We did not end up with any children because the umbilical cord was separate from the wall of the uterus in the second trimester. This happened three times and it was very hard on both of us. First of all, they put us in the same floor with all the others who had delivered with lots of laughter and balloons, etc. We did not think it was good for her long term health.

In the meantime, I was always looking for a better job that I would be happy about and could offer a long time career. In late 1970, Michelin Tire offered me a position as a full time recruiter. As part of the early training, they sent me to Baltimore, Maryland to call on tire dealers and large trucking companies. They just finished the United States facility in Greenville, South Carolina where passenger tires were manufactured. The plant in Anderson manufactured the rubber compounds.

Michelin's only customer in the United States in 1971 was Sears who carried the tires that were made in South Carolina. There were several more plants in the future. The biggest problem was finding potential employees who would stick it out through rigorous training and make a career at Michelin.

After three weeks in Baltimore, introducing myself as Robert Waterman with Michelin, explaining what kind of tire it is to retail passenger dealers and local based over the road trucking companies; I went back to New York for two months of rigorous training. When I spoke to the dealers or trucking company and gave them the Michelin name, the response was what kind of tire is a Michigan tire? No one knew who I was representing. After I finished field training, I was assigned to Chicago, Illinois. A warehouse would be built there and that was my office as well. I was given full hiring authority for sales representatives, warehouse managers, and product engineers. My territory started in Pittsburgh, Pennsylvania and went across the northern half of the United States to the Pacific Ocean, as well as the western four provinces of Canada.

I visited employment agencies in all major cities and always attended Lenman Weekend for opportunities to interview and hire separating military officers. Michelin never paid the most in starting income but fringe benefits galore that lasted a lifetime. They are still paying me. I held this position for eight years and hired some of the people who climbed corporate ladders and ran the company. That was the best payday for me. Knowing the ones that I picked out ended up running Michelin North America. The company was foreign and demanding on me and everyone else but what a thrill to see the results.

My wife was diagnosed with pancreatic cancer and Michelin paid every cent. I was allowed to choose not to come to work so I could take care of her. Her mom would come from time to time and stay a while. I went to work but was just about useless. Michelin kept me on and paid me. She died eleven months later. We had been married for twenty three years. I went back to work and the manager at Michelin America Research Development Company welcomed me home to my job. There would be no penalties for all the time not on the job. They gave me a simple tracking job on a computer with a D-Base software. No challenge; read books and balance checkbook.

Finally, I asked for a separation. They responded generously because I always received good reviews for all my twenty years of service. After almost five years, I married my wife Marcia in 1991. We have been together for the last thirty-three years. She also worked at Michelin and that was the major factor allowing my departure. I had benefits through her.

When I left Michelin, I told Marcia I was taking a year off. I was fifty years old and had worked all my life. Marcia started her campaign to help me decide what was next. I had bought a couple of small houses, remodeled them, and sold them at a profit. She pushed me into real estate sales. After two months, I realized that I lacked everything to get listings. Because I relocated here from New York, I had no circle of influence here. You have to be known and I was not. I only worked at Michelin and did not attend the schools and colleges in the area. I was ready to resign.

A friend showed me an article that discussed a buyer agency. I went to see a successful buyer agent in Columbia and spent the whole day with him. I decided to start my own real estate business, Buyers Only Realty. I received my mortgage broker license. The first three years were slow. Then those asking for my help increased, and several came back to purchase with upgrades. I ask my wife to resign from Michelin to help me and she did. We became top producers and kept it up for fifteen years and retired at sixty five.

The Army gave me a whole new beginning, with a chance to rewrite my vision of what my life could be. I loved it and will always be grateful to the Army for the doors that opened for me and the hope for the future that the Army gave me.

I was so impressed by the Hospice workers who took care of my first wife, I have spent the last sixteen years in service to the terminally ill. I volunteer for Hospice and Richard Campbell Veterans Hospital. God gave me the grace needed to take care of those who need help to get through each day. I look forward to helping others through Vets Helping Vets Anderson.

Honor and Mourn

In every land vets have stood watch
to keep our homeland safe, topnotch.

Some days mundane, some days insane,
in desert suns, in pouring rains.

Fought musket-to-musket with bayonets.
They met in fields to defeat the threats.

Faced snow and frostbite under Washington.
They destroyed Al-Qaeda in Desert Storm.

They hit beaches running, watched buddies fall,
but kept storming past those who gave all.

They crawled through mud and slept on rocks,
surrounded by snipers and jungle rot.

By Jay Wright, FWG

Jay Wright
Foothills Writers Guild Historian

Veteran's Day is for honoring and thanking living veterans for their contribution to our national security and many freedoms. However, Memorial Day is a somber day to honor and mourn those who died in or as the result of battle. A day to place flowers or flags on military graves; to pause for prayer or a moment of silence for those who gave all.

I had the privilege of serving in the Naval Air Force in Florida and in Sicily during the Vietnam Era. I met patriots from every branch of service who'd served in submarines, helicopters, foxholes, carriers, fighter aircraft, chow halls, troop transport, equipment maintenance, intel operations, etc. I listened to big, bad soldiers weep openly about the loss of a buddy from enemy fire, equipment explosion, or torture as a P.O.W. In spite of the beers and tears, PTSD is a reality for many today.

Conclusion

At the very beginning of the veterans' book project in 2021, Jim Godfrey, a Navy veteran, handed me a small box of memorabilia that once belonged to a WWII veteran. Inside the shoe box were medals, personal notes, and a few old photographs. He discovered the box in a storage shed while cleaning out his mother-in-law's home. Jim said that the veteran was a friend of the family and deserved recognition for his service.

Opening the box, I found a small but important portion of one man's life. His name was Harry L. Moore. He passed in Anderson, South Carolina on December 21, 2018, at ninety-four. Moore entered the United States Army at age seventeen in 1941 and left a few hand-written notes about his service. As I read some of Moore's notes written in cursive handwriting, I wondered how many younger students would be able to read his written words. Cursive writing is almost obsolete. We must remember that it was used to record much of our historical documents.

Harry L. Moore was born in Washington, Pennsylvania on November 25, 1924. He was the son of Paul and Mildred Moore. Moore notes that his mother had six sons in WWII. Four of the sons were in combat at one time. Harry's dog-tags bear the stamp of his mother's name, Mildred Moore, and her residence, Wolfdale, Pennsylvania. The dog-tags were stamped with T43, which means he received his tetanus shot in 1943 and a "P" showing he was of the Protestant faith. The military removed personal information from dog-tags in 1943 to protect captured soldiers.

Moore served three years in the Pacific area during WWII and later wrote these notes initialed HM: *Three hundred of us (recruits) left Washington on a train for Fort Meade, Maryland. We were all from the Washington area and stayed pretty much together in what became the 501st and 502nd Anti-Aircraft Battalions. We left Fort Meade and went to Camp Edwards, Massachusetts, where we went through Basic Training. We then shipped out to Pearl Harbor, where we set up on Ford Island (in the middle of Pearl Harbor) and protected the Island while we took amphibians and jungle training. The following is a day-by-day record from that time until we came home. We were not allowed to have diaries, but some did keep one. I kept most of the blood and gut events out of my diaries for fear of getting caught and rigorously punished for having violated the rule, but some of the happenings were described pretty well.*

Note: We shot down and got credit for 132 jap planes. Including the last plane shot down in WWII. We got a Presidential citation for killing 1300 japs and knocking out nine tanks in one night. I have record of the number of enemy plane attacks we had and the number of artillery rounds (45lbs.) we fired. We used 90 MM guns for artillery and anti-aircraft action.

Moore wrote he was with the soldiers who went in on the first wave (landing) of both operations in Leyte, Philippines and Okinawa. He was awarded the U.S. Army 24th Corps Arrowhead patch and the 7th Hourglass Division patch. He received three Purple Hearts during his service. His note reads: *I received one wound at Pearl Harbor, three wounds at Leyte, and one wound in Okinawa, but I told them one Purple Heart is enough. Our group suffered thirty-two percent casualties in one battery the night of the invasion at Leyte.*

Moore also stated he saw General Douglas MacArthur as he landed on Leyte on the General's "return" to the Philippines. As a young soldier, Moore stood Honor Guard for President Franklin Roosevelt when he inspected the troops in Hawaii and was recorded on the newsreel of the event. This took place just before the President died April 12, 1945. Moore's unit was loading up for attack on Japan's mainland when the war ended. He is recorded to have fought in ten of the most important battles in WWII, including Attu, Kiska, Kwajalein, Leyte, and Okinawa, and was awarded the Asian-Pacific Medal.

If we do not preserve this and other soldiers' stories, the generations to come will lose a crucial part of history. Only a few notes were in the box. I tell the story to remind each of us to document and preserve each of our veteran's mementos. They will prove valuable in the future to families, friends, and historians who want to know accurate history.

I hope that each of you reading *Vets Helping Vets Anderson: In Their Own Words,* Volumes I and II will help preserve our veterans' stories. The men and women in uniform, past or present, are the true Patriots. They love the United States of America and know firsthand that freedom is not free; lives were sacrificed, and lives were changed. Start the conversation today, ask the questions, document their answers. Help preserve history! **Angela Mason Lowe**

About the Author

Angela Mason Lowe became a Foothills Writers Guild member in the fall of 2018. She was elected chair for the term 2023-2024. Angela's journey as a writer began through a poetry class at Anderson University's Lifelong Learning Institute. In 2019, she compiled a book of poems and stories of Norman Cleveland Mason, *Tales of Lost Loves and Unusual Occurrences.* She also compiled a book of her poems, *Full of Grace and Grit.*

January 1, 2020, Angela resurrected the Pegasus Poets Chapter of the FWG. For the next two years, she faithfully sent out 105 prompts to fifteen poets of FWG. From the collection of poems written by Pegasus poets, she compiled a book, *Soaring:2021 Poems by Pegasus Poets II.* She is proud to say the chapter is still going strong today.

In 2022, Angela compiled a book from the suggestion of her husband, Tommy Lowe; *Vets Helping Vets Anderson: In Their Own Words.* She completed the *Vets Helping Vets Anderson: In Their Own Words Volume II* in 2023. Angela is passionate about preserving and documenting history. She inspires others to tell their story in their own words. Whether it is a story or poem, Angela's heart-felt expression of the hard-working textile mill family of bygone days, the farmer who tries to save the family farm, and the veteran who served their country in war or peace tugs at the readers emotions.

Angela's accolades include: 2019 Backstreet Press Horizon Award and Pacesetter's Award for accomplishing a lot in the short time of being a poet and writer; 2020 FWG

Story of the Year Award and FWG scholarship; and 2021 Backstreet Pacesetter Award for writing leadership, and FWG Writing Contest Gallery Bronze Award.

She will humbly tell you her greatest reward is the gratitude of those she writes about. Her goal is to light a torch for others to take the time to listen to and document other people's stories. When she is not writing, Angela volunteers for Hospice of the Upstate and Wives of Vets Helping Vets Anderson and plays ukulele with the Happy Strummers. The Governor appointed her to the Pendleton District Historical, Recreational and Tourism Commission of South Carolina in 2014. Angela presently serves as the chair for the Commission, promoting and preserving history. In her own words, "Written words preserve the picture, for time has a way of fading, even a masterpiece."

She and her husband live in Anderson, South Carolina. Their daughter Amber Lowe Moeckel and her two children, Audrie and Jacob live close by. Their son Erick Mason Lowe and his wife Hannah-Grace manage their Mason Century Farm in Oakway, South Carolina.

Contact Angela: Graceandgrit@bellsouth.net

Made in the USA
Columbia, SC
22 May 2024

35603699R00165